THE PRINCE

By NICCOLÒ MACHIAVELLI

Translated by
NINIAN HILL THOMSON

Introduction by HENRY CUST

The Prince
By Niccolò Machiavelli
Translated by Ninian Hill Thomson
Introduction by Henry Cust

Print ISBN 13: 978-1-4209-5190-5
eBook ISBN 13: 978-1-4209-5191-2

Cover Image: Portrait of Niccolò Machiavelli (Florence, 1469 - Florence, 1527), Italian historian, writer, playwright, politician and philosopher, Oil on board by Santi di Tito (1536-1606), 104x85 cm / De Agostini Picture Library / Bridgeman Images.

Please visit *www.digireads.com*

CONTENTS

Introduction

'I am at my farm; and, since my last misfortunes, have not been in Florence twenty days. I spent September in snaring thrushes; but at the end of the month, even this rather tiresome sport failed me. I rise with the sun, and go into a wood of mine that is being cut, where I remain two hours inspecting the work of the previous day and conversing with the woodcutters, who have always some trouble on hand amongst themselves or with their neighbors. When I leave the wood, I go to a spring, and thence to the place which I use for snaring birds, with a book under my arm—Dante or Petrarch, or one of the minor poets, like Tibullus or Ovid. I read the story of their passions, and let their loves remind me of my own, which is a pleasant pastime for a while. Next I take the road, enter the inn door, talk with the passers-by, inquire the news of the neighborhood, listen to a variety of matters, and make note of the different tastes and humors of men.

This brings me to dinner-time, when I join my family and eat the poor produce of my farm. After dinner I go back to the inn, where I generally find the host and a butcher, a miller, and a pair of bakers. With these companions I play the fool all day at cards or backgammon: a thousand squabbles, a thousand insults and abusive dialogues take place, while we haggle over a farthing, and shout loud enough to be heard from San Casciano.

But when evening falls I go home and enter my writing-room. On the threshold I put off my country habits, filthy with mud and mire, and array myself in royal courtly garments. Thus worthily attired, I make my entrance into the ancient courts of the men of old, where they receive me with love, and where I feed upon that food which only is my own and for which I was born. I feel no shame in conversing with them and asking them the reason of their actions.

They, moved by their humanity, make answer. For four hours' space I feel no annoyance, forget all care; poverty cannot frighten, nor death appal me. I am carried away to their society. And since Dante says "that there is no science unless we retain what we have learned" I have set down what I have gained from their discourse, and composed a treatise, *De Principatibus*, in which I enter as deeply as I can into the science of the subject, with reasonings on the nature of principality, its several species, and how they are acquired, how maintained, how lost. If you ever liked any of my scribblings, this ought to suit your taste. To a prince, and especially to a new prince, it ought to prove acceptable. Therefore I am dedicating it to the Magnificence of Giuliano.'

Such is the account that Niccolò Machiavelli renders of himself when after imprisonment, torture, and disgrace, at the age of forty-four, he first turned to serious writing. For the first twenty-six or indeed twenty-nine of those years we have not one line from his pen or one word of vaguest information about him. Throughout all his works written for publication, there is little news about himself. Montaigne could properly write, 'Ainsi, lecteur, je suis moy-mesme la matière de mon livre.' But the matter of Machiavelli was far other: 'Io ho espresso quanto io so, e quanto io ho imparato per una lunga pratica e continua lezione delle cose del mondo.'

Machiavelli was born on the 3rd of May 1469. The period of his life almost exactly coincides with that of Cardinal Wolsey. He came of the old and noble Tuscan stock of Montespertoli, who were men of their hands in the eleventh century. He carried their coat, but the property had been wasted and divided. His forefathers had held office of high distinction, but had fallen away as the new wealth of the bankers and traders increased in Florence. He himself inherited a small property in San Casciano and its neighborhood, which assured him a sufficient, if somewhat lean, independence. Of his education we know little enough. He was well acquainted with Latin, and knew, perhaps, Greek enough to serve his turn. Rather not 'without letters than lettered,' Varchi describes him. That he was not loaded down with learned reading proved probably a great advantage. The coming of the French, and the expulsion of the Medici, the proclamation of the Republic (1494), and later the burning of Savonarola convulsed Florence and threw open many public offices. It has been suggested, but without much foundation, that some clerical work was found for Machiavelli in 1494 or even earlier. It is certain that on July 14, 1498, he was appointed Chancellor and Secretary to the Dieci di Libertà e Pace, an office which he held till the close of his political life at fall of the Republic in 1512.

The functions of his Council were extremely varied, and in the hands of their Secretary became yet more diversified. They represented in some sense the Ministry for Home, Military, and especially for Foreign Affairs. It is impossible to give any full account of Machiavelli's official duties. He wrote many thousands of despatches and official letters, which are still preserved. He was on constant errands of State through the Florentine dominions. But his diplomatic missions and what he learned by them make the main interest of his office. His first adventure of importance was to the Court of Caterina Sforza, the Lady of Forlì, in which matter that astute Countess entirely bested the teacher of all diplomatists to be. In 1500 he smelt powder at the siege at Pisa, and was sent to France to allay the irritations of Louis XII. Many similar and lesser missions follow. The results are in no case of great importance, but the opportunities to the Secretary of learning men and things, intrigue and policy, the Court and the gutter were invaluable. At the camp of Caesar Borgia, in 1502, he found in his host that fantastic hero whom he incarnated in *The Prince*, and he was practically an eyewitness of the amazing masterpiece, the Massacre of Sinigaglia. The next year he is sent to Rome with a watching brief at the election of Julius II, and in 1506 is again sent to negotiate with the Pope. An embassy to the Emperor Maximilian, a second mission to the French King at Blois, in which he persuades Louis XII to postpone the threatened General Council of the Church (1511), and constant expeditions to report upon and set in order unrestful towns and provinces did not fulfil his activity. His pen was never idle. Reports, despatches, elaborate monographs on France, Germany, or wherever he might be, and personal letters innumerable, and even yet unpublished, ceased not night nor day. Detail, wit, character-drawing, satire, sorrow, bitterness, all take their turn. But this was only a fraction of his work. By duty and by expediency he was bound to follow closely the internal politics of Florence where his enemies and rivals abounded. And in all these years he was pushing forward and carrying through with unceasing and unspeakable vigor the great military dream of his life, the foundation of a National Militia and the extinction of Mercenary Companies. But the fabric he had fancied and thought to have built proved unsubstantial. The spoilt half-mutinous levies whom he had spent years in odious and unwilling training failed him at the crowning moment in strength and spirit: and the fall of the Republic implied the fall of Machiavelli and the close of his official life. He struggled hard to save himself, but the wealthy classes were against him, perhaps afraid of him, and on them the Medici relied. For a year he was forbidden to leave Florentine territory, and for a while was excluded from the Palazzo. Later his name was found in a list of Anti-Medicean conspirators. He was arrested and decorously tortured with six turns of the rack, and then liberated for want of evidence.

For perhaps a year after his release the Secretary engaged in a series of tortuous intrigues to gain the favor of the Medici. Many of the stories may be exaggerated, but none make pleasant reading, and nothing proved successful. His position was miserable. Temporarily crippled by torture, out of favor with the Government, shunned by his friends, in deep poverty, burdened with debt and with a wife and four children, his material circumstances were ill enough. But, worse still, he was idle. He had deserved well of the Republic, and had never despaired of it, and this was his reward. He seemed to himself a broken man. He had no great natural dignity, no great moral strength. He profoundly loved and admired Dante, but he could not for one moment imitate him. He sought satisfaction in sensuality of life and writing, but found no comfort. Great things were stirring in the world and he had

neither part nor lot in them. By great good fortune he began a
correspondence with his friend Francesco Vettori, the Medicean
Ambassador at Rome, to whom he appeals for his good offices; 'And if
nothing can be done, I must live as I came into the world, for I was
born poor and learnt to want before learning to enjoy.' Before long
these two diplomats had co-opted themselves into a kind of Secret
Cabinet of Europe. It is a strange but profoundly interesting
correspondence, both politically and personally. Nothing is too great or
too small, too glorious or too mean for their pens. Amid foolish
anecdotes and rather sordid love affairs the politics of Europe, and
especially of Italy, are dissected and discussed. Leo X had now plunged
into political intrigue. Ferdinand of Spain was in difficulty. France had
allied herself with Venice. The Swiss are the Ancient Romans, and may
conquer Italy. Then back again, or rather constant throughout, the love
intrigues and the 'likely wench hard-by who may help to pass our
time.' But through it all there is an ache at Machiavelli's heart, and on a
sudden he will break down, crying,

> Pero se alcuna volta io rido e canto
> Facciol, perchè non ho Be non quest' una
> Via da sfogare il mio angoscioso pianto.

Vettori promised much, but nothing came of it. By 1515 the
correspondence died away, and the Ex-Secretary found for himself at
last the true pathway through his vale of years.

The remainder of Machiavelli's life is bounded by his books. He
settled at his villa at San Casciano, where he spent his day as he
describes in the letter quoted at the beginning of this essay. In 1518 he
began to attend the meetings of the Literary Club in the Orti Oricellarii,
and made new and remarkable friends. 'Era amato grandemente da loro
. . . e della sua conversazione si dilettavano maravigliosamente,
tenendo in prezzo grandissimo tutte l'opere sue,' which shows the
personal authority he exercised. Occasionally he was employed by
Florentine merchants to negotiate for them at Venice, Genoa, Lucca,
and other places. In 1519 Cardinal Medici deigned to consult him as to
the Government, and commissioned him to write the History of
Florence. But in the main he wrote his books and lived the daily life we
know. In 1525 he went to Rome to present his History to Clement VII,
and was sent on to Guicciardini. In 1526 he was busy once more with
military matters and the fortification of Florence. On the 22nd of June
1527 he died at Florence immediately after the establishment of the
second Republic. He had lived as a practising Christian, and so died,
surrounded by his wife and family. Wild legends grew about his death,
but have no foundation. A peasant clod in San Casciano could not have
made a simpler end. He was buried in the family Chapel in Santa

Croce, and a monument was there at last erected with the epitaph by Doctor Ferroni—'Tanto nomini nullum par elogium.' The first edition of his complete works was published in 1782, and was dedicated to Lord Cowper.

What manner of man was Machiavelli at home and in the market-place? It is hard to say. There are doubtful busts, the best, perhaps, that engraved in the 'Testina' edition of 1550, so-called on account of the portrait. 'Of middle height, slender figure, with sparkling eyes, dark hair, rather a small head, a slightly aquiline nose, a tightly closed mouth: all about him bore the impress of a very acute observer and thinker, but not that of one able to wield much influence over others.' Such is a reconstruction of him by one best able to make one. 'In his conversation,' says Varchi, 'Machiavelli was pleasant, serviceable to his friends, a friend of virtuous men, and, in a word, worthy to have received from Nature either less genius or a better mind.' If not much above the moral standard of the day he was certainly not below it. His habits were loose and his language lucid and licentious. But there is no bad or even unkind act charged against him. To his honesty and good faith he very fairly claims that his poverty bears witness. He was a kind, if uncertain, husband and a devoted father. His letters to his children are charming. Here is one written soon before his death to his little son Guido.—'Guido, my darling son, I received a letter of thine and was delighted with it, particularly because you tell me of your full recovery, the best news I could have. If God grants life to us both I expect to make a good man of you, only you must do your fair share yourself. Guido is to stick to his books and music, and if the family mule is too fractious, Unbridle him, take off the halter and turn him loose at Montepulciano. The farm is large, the mule is small, so no harm can come of it. Tell your mother, with my love, not to be nervous. I shall surely be home before any trouble comes. Give a kiss to Baccina, Piero, and Totto: I wish I knew his eyes were getting well. Be happy and spend as little as you may. Christ have you in his keeping.'—There is nothing exquisite or divinely delicate in this letter, but there are many such, and they were not written by a bad man, any more than the answers they evoke were addressed to one. There is little more save of a like character that is known of Machiavelli the man. But to judge him and his work we must have some knowledge of the world in which he was to move and have his being.

At the beginning of the sixteenth century Italy was rotten to the core. In the close competition of great wickedness the Vicar of Christ easily carried off the palm, and the Court of Alexander VI was probably the wickedest meeting-place of men that has ever existed upon earth. No virtue, Christian or Pagan, was there to be found; little art that was not sensuous or sensual. It seemed as if Bacchus and Venus and Priapus had come to their own again, and yet Rome had not ceased to call herself Christian.

'Owing to the evil ensample of the Papal Court,' writes Machiavelli, 'Italy has lost all piety and all religion: whence follow infinite troubles and disorders; for as religion implies all good, so its absence implies the contrary. To the Church and priests of Rome we owe another even greater disaster which is the cause of her ruin. I mean that the Church has maintained, and still maintains Italy divided.' The Papacy is too weak to unite and rule, but strong enough to prevent others doing so, and is always ready to call in the foreigner to crush all Italians to the foreigner's profit, and Guicciardini, a high Papal officer, commenting on this, adds, It would be impossible to speak so ill of the Roman Court, but that more abuse should not be merited, seeing it is an infamy, and example of all the shames and scandals of the world.' The lesser clergy, the monks, the nuns followed, with anxious fidelity, the footsteps of their shepherds. There was hardly a tonsure in Italy which covered more than thoughts and hopes of lust and avarice. Religion and morals which God had joined together, were set by man a thousand leagues asunder. Yet religion still sat upon the alabaster throne of Peter, and in the filthy straw of the meanest Calabrian confessional. And still deeper remained a blind devoted superstition. Vitellozzo Vitelli, as Machiavelli tells us, while being strangled by Caesar Borgia's assassin, implored his murderer to procure for him the absolution of that murderer's father. Gianpaolo Baglioni, who reigned by parricide and lived in incest, was severely blamed by the Florentines for not killing Pope JuliusII when the latter was his guest at Perugia. And when Gabrino Fondato, the tyrant of Cremona, was on the scaffold, his only regret was that when he had taken his guests, the Pope and Emperor, to the top of the Cremona tower, four hundred feet high, his nerve failed him and he did not push them both over. Upon this anarchy of religion, morals, and conduct breathed suddenly the inspiring breath of Pagan antiquity which seemed to the Italian mind to find its finest climax in tyrannicide. There is no better instance than in the plot of the Pazzi at Florence. Francesco Pazzi and Bernardo Bandini decided to kill Lorenzo and Giuliano de' Medici in the cathedral at the moment of the elevation of the Host. They naturally took the priest into their confidence. They escorted Giuliano to the Duomo, laughing, and talking, and playfully embraced him—to discover if he wore armor under his clothes. Then they killed him at the moment appointed.

Nor were there any hills from which salvation might be looked for. Philosophy, poetry, science, expressed themselves in terms of materialism. Faith and hope are ever the last survivors in the life of a man or of a nation. But in Italy these brave comforters were at their latest breath. It is perhaps unfair to accept in full the judgment of Northern travellers. The conditions, training, needs of England and

Germany were different. In these countries courage was a necessity, and good faith a paying policy. Subtlety could do little against a two-handed sword in the hands of an angry or partially intoxicated giant. Climate played its part as well as culture, and the crude pleasures and vices of the North seemed fully as loathsome to the refined Italian as did the tortuous policy and the elaborate infamies of the South to their rough invaders. Alone, perhaps, among the nations of Europe the Italians had never understood or practised chivalry, save in such select and exotic schools as the Casa Gioiosa under Vittorino da Feltre at Mantua. The oath of Arthur's knights would have seemed to them mere superfluity of silliness. *Onore* connoted credit, reputation, and prowess. *Virtù*, which may be roughly translated as mental ability combined with personal daring, set the standard and ruled opinion. 'Honor in the North was subjective: *Onore* in Italy objective.' Individual liberty, indeed, was granted in full to all, at the individual's risk. The love of beauty curbed grossness and added distinction. Fraud became an art and force a science. There is liberty for all, but for the great ones there is licence. And when the day of trial comes, it is the Churchmen and the Princes who can save neither themselves nor man, nor thing that is theirs. To such a world was Machiavelli born. To whom should he turn? To the People? To the Church? To the Princes and Despots? But hear him:—

'There shall never be found any good mason, which will believe to be able to make a fair image of a piece of marble ill-hewed, but very well of a rude piece. Our Italian Princes believed, before they tasted the blows of the outlandish war, that it should suffice a Prince to know by writings, how to make a subtle answer, to write a goodly letter, to show in sayings, and in words, wit and promptness, to know how to canvas a fraud, to deck themselves with precious stones and gold, to sleep and to eat with greater glory then other: To keep many lascivious persons about them, to govern themselves with their subjects, covetously and proudly: To root in idleness, to give the degrees of the exercise of war, for good will, to despise if any should have showed them any laudable way, minding that their words should be answers of oracles: nor the silly wretches were not aware that they prepared themselves to be a pray to whom so ever should assault them. Hereby grew then in the thousand four hundred and ninety and four year, the great fears, the sudden flights and the marvelous losses: and so three most mighty states which were in Italy, have bene diverse times sacked and destroyed. But that which is worse, is where those that remain, continue in the very same error, and live in the very same disorder and consider not, that those who in old time would keep their states, caused to be done these things, which of me hath been reasoned, and that their studies were, to prepare the body to diseases, and the mind not to fear perils. Whereby grew that Caesar, Alexander, and all those men and excellent Princes in old time, were the foremost amongst the fighters, going armed on foot: and if they lost their state, they would lose their life, so that they lived and died virtuously.'

Such was the clay that waited the moulding of the potter's hand. 'Posterity, that high court of appeal, which is never tired of eulogizing its own justice and discernment,' has recorded harsh sentence on the Florentine. It is better today to let him speak for himself.

The slender volume of *The Prince* has probably produced wider discussion, more bitter controversy, more varied interpretations and a deeper influence than any book save Holy Writ. Kings and statesmen, philosophers and theologians, monarchists and republicans have all and always used or abused it for their purposes. Written in 1513, the first year of Machiavelli's disgrace, concurrently with part of the *Discorsi*, which contain the germs of it, the book represents the fullness of its author's thought and experience. It was not till after Machiavelli's death, that it was published in 1532, by order of Clement VII. Meanwhile, however, in manuscript it had been widely read and favorably received.

The mere motive of its creation and dedication has been the theme of many volumes. Machiavelli was poor, was idle, was out of favor, and therefore, though a Republican, wrote a devilish hand-book of tyranny to strengthen the Medici and recover his position. Machiavelli, a loyal Republican, wrote a primer of such fiendish principles as might lure the Medici to their ruin. Machiavelli's one idea was to ruin the rich: Machiavelli's one idea was to oppress the poor: he was a Protestant, a Jesuit, an Atheist: a Royalist and a Republican. And the book published by one Pope's express authority was utterly condemned and forbidden, with all its author's works, by the express command of another (1559). But before facing the whirlwind of savage controversy which raged and rages still about *The Prince*, it may be well to consider shortly the book itself—consider it as a new book and without prejudice. The purpose of its composition is almost certainly to be found in the plain fact that Machiavelli, a politician and a man of letters, wished to write a book upon the subject which had been his special study and lay nearest to his business and bosom. To ensure prominence for such a book, to engage attention and incidentally perhaps to obtain political employment for himself, he dedicated it to Lorenzo de' Medici, the existing and accepted Chief of the State. But far and above such lighter motives stood the fact that he saw in Lorenzo the only man who might conceivably bring to being the vast dream of patriotism which the writer had imagined. The subject he proposed to himself was largely, though not wholly, conditioned by the time and place in which he lived. He wrote for his countrymen and he wrote for his own generation. He had heard with his ears and seen with his eyes the alternate rending anarchy and moaning paralysis of Italy. He had seen what Agricola had long before been spared the sight of. And what he saw, he saw not through a glass darkly or distorted, but in the whitest, driest light, without flinching and face to face. 'We are much beholden,' writes Bacon, 'to Machiavelli and others that wrote what men do, and not what they ought to do.' He did not despair of Italy, he did not despair even of Italian unity. But he despaired of what he saw around him, and he was willing at almost any price to end it. He recognized, despite the nominal example of Venice, that a Republican system was impossible, and that the small Principalities and Free Cities were corrupt beyond hope of healing. A strong central unifying government was imperative, and at that day such government could only be vested in a single man. For it must ever be closely remembered, as will be pointed out again, that throughout the book the Prince is what would now be called the Government. And then he saw with faithful prophecy, in the splendid peroration of his hope, a hope deferred for near four hundred years, he saw beyond the painful paths of blood and tyranny, a vision of deliverance and union. For at least it is plain that in all things Machiavelli was a passionate patriot, and *Amo la patria mia più dell' anima* is found in one of the last of many thousand letters that his untiring pen had written.

The purpose, then, of *The Prince* is to lay down rules, within the possibilities of the time, for the making of a man who shall create, increase, and maintain a strong and stable government. This is done in the main by a plain presentation of facts, a presentation condensed and critical but based on men and things as they actually were. The ethical side is wholly omitted: the social and economical almost entirely. The aspect is purely political, with the underlying thought, it may be supposed, that under the postulated government, all else will prosper.

Machiavelli opens by discussing the various forms of governments, which he divides into Republics and Principalities. Of the latter some may be hereditary and some acquired. Of hereditary states he says little and quotes but one, the Duchy of Ferrara. He then turns to his true subject, the acquisition and preservation of States wholly new or new in part, States such as he saw himself on every side around him. Having gained possession of a new State, he says, you must first extirpate the family of your predecessor. You should then either reside or plant colonies, but not trust to garrisons. 'Colonies are not costly to the Prince, are more faithful and cause less offence to the subject States: those whom they may injure being poor and scattered, are prevented from doing mischief. should be observed that men ought either to be caressed or trampled out, seeing that small injuries may be avenged, whereas great ones destroy the possibility of retaliation: and so the damage that has to be inflicted ought to be such that it need involve no fear of reprisals.' There is perhaps in all Machiavelli no better example of his lucid scientific method than this passage. There is neither excuse nor hypocrisy. It is merely a matter of business calculation. Mankind is the raw material, the State is the finished work. Further you are to conciliate your neighbors who are weak and abase the strong, and you must not let the stranger within your gates. Above all look before as well as after and think not to leave it to time, *godere li benefici del tempo*, but, as did the Romans, strike and strike at once. For illustration he criticizes, in a final and damning analysis, the career of Louis XII in Italy. There was no canon of statecraft so absolute that the King did not ignore it, and in inevitable Nemesis, there was no ultimate disaster so crowning as not to be achieved.

After observing that a feudal monarchy is much less easy of conquest than a despotism, since in the one case you must vanquish many lesser lordships while in the other you merely replace slaves by slaves, Machiavelli considers the best method of subjugating Free Cities. Here again is eminent the terrible composure and the exact truth of his politics. A conquered Free City you may of course rule in person, or you may construct an oligarchy to govern for you, but the only safe way is to destroy it utterly, since 'that name of Liberty, those ancient usages of Freedom,' are things which no length of years and no benefits can extinguish in the nation's mind, things which no pains or forethought can uproot unless the citizens be utterly destroyed.'

Hitherto the discussion has ranged round the material politics of the matter, the acquisition of material power. Machiavelli now turns to the heart of his matter, the proper character and conduct of a new Prince in a new Principality and the ways by which he shall deal most fortunately with friend and foe. For fortune it is, as well as ability, which go to the making of the man and the maintenance of his power.

In the manner of the day Moses, Cyrus, Romulus, and Theseus are led across the stage in illustration. The common attribute of all such fortunate masters of men was force of arms, while the mission of an unarmed prophet such as Savonarola was foredoomed to failure. In such politics Machiavelli is positive and ruthless: force is and must be the remedy and the last appeal, a principle which indeed no later generation has in practice set at naught. But in the hard dry eyes of the Florentine Secretary stood, above all others, one shining figure, a figure to all other eyes, from then till now, wrapped in mysterious and miasmatic cloud. In the pages of common history he was a tyrant, he was vicious beyond compare, he was cruel beyond the Inquisition, he was false beyond the Father of Lies, he was the Antichrist of Rome and he was a failure: but he was the hero of Niccolò Machiavelli, who, indeed, found in Caesar Borgia the fine flower of Italian politics in the Age of the Despots. Son of the Pope, a Prince of the Church, a Duke of France, a master of events, a born soldier, diplomatist, and more than half a statesman, Caesar seemed indeed the darling of gods and men whom original fortune had crowned with inborn ability. Machiavelli knew him as well as it was possible to know a soul so tortuous and secret, and he had been present at the most critical and terrible moments of Caesar's life. That in despite of a life which the world calls infamous, in despite of the howling execrations of all Christendom, in despite of ultimate and entire failures, Machiavelli could still write years after, 'I know not what lessons I could teach a new Prince more useful than the example of his actions,' exhibits the ineffaceable impressions that Caesar Borgia had made upon the most subtle and observant mind of modern history.

Caesar was the acknowledged son of Pope Alexander by his acknowledged mistress Vannozza dei Cattani. Born in 1472, he was an Archbishop and a Cardinal at sixteen, and the murderer of his elder brother at an age when modern youths are at college. He played his part to the full in the unspeakable scandals of the Vatican, but already 'he spoke little and people feared him.' Ere long the splendors of the Papacy seemed too remote and uncertain for his fierce ambition, and, indeed, through his father, he already wielded both the temporal and the spiritual arms of Peter. To the subtlety of the Italian his Spanish blood had lent a certain stern resolution, and as with Julius and Sulla the lust for sloth and sensuality were quickened by the lust for sway. He unfrocked himself with pleasure. He commenced politician, soldier, and despot. And for the five years preceding Alexander's death he may almost be looked upon as a power in Europe. Invested Duke of Romagna, that hot-bed of petty tyranny and tumult, he repressed disorder through his governor Messer Ramiro with a relentless hand. When order reigned, Machiavelli tells us he walked out one morning into the market-place at Cesena and saw the body of Ramiro, who had borne the odium of reform, lying in two pieces with his head on a lance, and a bloody axe by his side. Caesar reaped the harvest of Ramiro's severity, and the people recognizing his benevolence and justice were 'astounded and satisfied.'

But the gaze of the Borgia was not bounded by the strait limits of a mere Italian Duchy. Whether indeed there mingled with personal ambition an ideal of a united Italy, swept clean of the barbarians, it is hard to say, though Machiavelli would have us believe it. What is certain is that he desired the supreme dominion in Italy for himself, and to win it spared neither force nor fraud nor the help of the very barbarians themselves. With a decree of divorce and a Cardinal's hat he gained the support of France, the French Duchy of Valentinois, and the sister of the King of Navarre to wife. By largesse of bribery and hollow promises he brought to his side the great families of Rome, his natural enemies, and the great Condottieri with their men-at-arms. When by their aid he had established and extended his government he mistrusted their good faith. With an infinity of fascination and cunning, without haste and without rest, he lured these leaders, almost more cunning than himself, to visit him as friends in his fortress of Sinigaglia. 'I doubt if they will be alive tomorrow morning,' wrote Machiavelli, who was on the spot. He was right. Caesar caused them to be strangled the same night, while his father dealt equal measure to their colleagues and adherents in Rome. Thenceforth, distrusting mercenaries, he found and disciplined, out of a mere rabble, a devoted army of his own, and having unobtrusively but completely extirpated the whole families of those whose thrones he had usurped, not only the present but the future seemed assured to him.

He had fulfilled the first of Machiavelli's four conditions. He rapidly achieved the remaining three. He bought the Roman nobles 'so as to be able to put a bridle in the new Pope's mouth.' He bought or poisoned or packed or terrorized the existing College of Cardinals and selected new Princes of the Church who should accept a Pontiff of his choosing. He was effectively strong enough to resist the first onset upon him at his father's death. Five years had been enough for so great an undertaking. One thing alone he had not and indeed could not have foreseen. 'He told me himself on the day on which (Pope) Julius was created, that he had foreseen and provided for everything else that could happen on his father's death, but had never anticipated that, when his father died, he too should have been at death's door.' Even so the fame and splendor of his name for a while maintained his authority against his unnumbered enemies. But soon the great betrayer was betrayed. 'It is well to cheat those who have been masters of treachery,' he had said himself in his hours of brief authority. His wheel had turned full cycle. Within three years his fate, like that of Charles XII, was destined to a foreign strand, a petty fortress, and a dubious hand. Given over to Spain he passed three years obscurely. 'He was struck down in a fight at Viana in Navarre (1507) after a furious resistance: he was stripped of his fine armor by men who did not know his name or quality and his body was left naked on the bare ground, bloody and riddled with wounds. He was only thirty-one.' And so the star of Machiavelli's hopes and dreams was quenched for a season in the clouds from which it came.

It seems worthwhile to sketch the strange tempestuous career of Caesar Borgia because in the remaining chapters of *The Prince* and elsewhere in his writings, it is the thought and memory of Valentinois, transmuted doubtless and idealized by the lapse of years, that largely inform and inspire the perfect Prince of Machiavelli. But it must not be supposed that in life or in mind they were intimate or even sympathetic. Machiavelli criticizes his hero liberally and even harshly. But for the work he wanted done he had found no better craftsman and no better example to follow for those that might come after. Morals and religion did not touch the purpose of his arguments except as affecting policy. In policy virtues may be admitted as useful agents and in the chapter following that on Caesar, entitled, curiously enough, 'Of those who by their crimes come to be Princes,' he lays down that to slaughter fellow citizens, to betray friends, to be devoid of honor, pity and religion cannot be counted as merits, for these are means which may lead to power but which confer no glory. Cruelty he would employ without hesitation but with the greatest care both in degree and in kind. It should be immediate and complete and leave no possibility of counter-revenge. For it is never forgotten by the living, and he deceives himself who believes that, with the great, recent benefits cause old wrongs to be forgotten.' On the other hand 'Benefits should be conferred little by little so that they may be more fully relished.' The cruelty proper to a Prince (Government, for as ever they are identical) aims only at authority. Now authority must spring from love or fear. It were best to combine both motives to obedience but you cannot. The Prince must remember that men are fickle, and love at their own pleasure, and that men are fearful and fear at the pleasure of the Prince. Let him therefore depend on what is of himself, not on that which is of others. 'Yet if he win not love he may escape hate, and so it will be if he does not meddle with the property or women-folk of his subjects.' When he must punish let him kill. 'For men will sooner forget the death of their father than the loss of their estate.' And moreover you cannot always go on killing, but a Prince who has once set himself to plundering will never stop. This is the more needful because the only secure foundation of his rule lies in his trust of the people and in their support. And indeed again and again you shall find no more thorough democrat than this teacher of tyrants. 'The people own better broader qualities, fidelities and passions than any Prince and have better cause to show for them.' 'As for prudence and stability, I say that a people is more stable, more prudent, and of better judgment than a Prince.' If the people go wrong it is almost certainly the crime or negligence of the Prince which drives or leads them astray. 'Better far than any number of fortresses is not to be hated by your people.' The support of the people and a national militia make the essential strength of the Prince and of the State.

The chapters on military organization may be more conveniently considered in conjunction with *The Art of War*. It is enough at present to point out two or three observations of Machiavelli which touch politics from the military side. To his generation they were entirely novel, though mere commonplace today. National strength means national stability and national greatness; and this can be achieved, and can only be achieved, by a national army. The Condottiere system, born of sloth and luxury, has proved its rottenness. Your hired general is either a tyrant or a traitor, a bully or a coward. 'In a word the armor of others is too wide or too strait for us: it falls off us, or it weighs us down.' And in a fine illustration he compares auxiliary troops to the armor of Saul which David refused, preferring to fight Goliath with his sling and stone.

Having assured the external security of the State, Machiavelli turns once more to the qualities and conduct of the Prince. So closely packed are these concluding chapters that it is almost impossible to compress them further. The author at the outset states his purpose: 'Since it is my object to write what shall be useful to whosoever understands it, it seems to me better to follow the practical truth of things rather than an imaginary view of them. For many Republics and Princedoms have been imagined that were never seen or known to exist in reality. And the manner in which we live and in which we ought to live, are things so wide asunder that he who suits the one to betake himself to the other is more likely to destroy than to save himself.' Nothing that Machiavelli wrote is more sincere, analytic, positive and ruthless. He operates unflinchingly on an assured diagnosis. The hand never an instant falters, the knife is never blunt. He deals with what is, and not with what ought to be. Should the Prince be all-virtuous, all-liberal, all-humane? Should his word be his bond forever? Should true religion be the master-passion of his life? Machiavelli considers. The first duty of the Prince (or Government) is to maintain the existence, stability, and prosperity of the State. Now if all the world were perfect so should the Prince be perfect too. But such are not the conditions of human life. An idealizing Prince must fall before a practicing world. A Prince must learn in self-defense how to be bad, but like Caesar Borgia, he must be a great judge of occasion. And what evil he does must be deliberate, appropriate, and calculated, and done, not selfishly, but for the good of the State of which he is trustee. There is the power of Law and the power of Force. The first is proper to men, the second to beasts. And that is why Achilles was brought up by Cheiron the Centaur that he might learn to use both natures. A ruler must be half lion and half fox, a fox to discern the toils, a lion to drive off the wolves. Merciful, faithful, humane, religious, just, these he may be and above all should seem to be, nor should any word escape his lips to give the lie to his professions: and in fact he should not leave these qualities but when he must. He should, if possible, practice goodness, but under necessity should know how to pursue evil. He should keep faith until occasion alter, or reason of state compel him to break his pledge. Above all he should profess and observe religion, 'because men in general judge rather by the eye than by the hand, and every one can see but few can touch.' But none the less, must he learn (as did William the Silent, Elizabeth of England, and Henry of Navarre) how to subordinate creed to policy when urgent need is upon him. In a word, he must realize and face his own position, and the facts of mankind and of the world. If not veracious to his conscience, he must be veracious to facts. He must not be bad for badness' sake, but seeing things as they are, must deal as he can to protect and preserve the trust committed to his care. Fortune is still a fickle jade, but at least the half our will is free, and if we are bold we may master her yet. For Fortune is a woman who, to be kept under, must be beaten and roughly handled, and we see that she is more ready to be mastered by those who treat her so, than by those who are shy in their wooing. And always, like a woman, she gives her favors to the young, because they are less scrupulous and fiercer and more audaciously command her to their will.

And so at the last the sometime Secretary of the Florentine Republic turns to the new Master of the Florentines in splendid exhortation. He points to no easy path. He proposes no mean ambition. He has said already that 'double will that Prince's glory be, who has founded a new realm and fortified it and adorned it with good laws, good arms, good friends, and good examples.' But there is more and better to be done. The great misery of men has ever made the great leaders of men. But was Israel in Egypt, were the Persians, the Athenians ever more enslaved, down-trodden, disunited, beaten, despoiled, mangled, over-run and desolate than is our Italy to-day? The barbarians must be hounded out, and Italy be free and one. Now is the accepted time. All Italy is waiting and only seeks the man. To you the darling of Fortune and the Church this splendid task is given, to you and to the army of Italy and of Italians only. Arm Italy and lead her. To you, the deliverer, what gates would be closed, what obedience refused! What jealousies opposed, what homage denied. Love, courage, and fixed fidelity await you, and under your standards shall the voice of Petrarch be fulfilled:

> Virtù contro al furore
> Prenderà l'arme e fia il combatter corto:
> Chè l'antico valore
> Negl' Italici cor non è ancor morto.

Such is *The Prince* of Machiavelli. The vision of its breathless exhortation seemed then as but a landscape to a blind man's eye. But the passing of three hundred and fifty years of the misery he wept for brought at the last, almost in perfect exactness, the fulfillment of that impossible prophecy.

There is no great book in the world of smaller compass than *The Prince* of Machiavelli. There is no book more lucidly, directly, and plainly written. There is no book that has aroused more vehement, venomous, and even truculent controversy from the moment of its publication until today. And it is asserted with great probability that *The Prince* has had a more direct action upon real life than any other book in the world, and a larger share in breaking the chains and lighting the dark places of the Middle Ages. It is a truism to say that Machiavelism existed before Machiavelli. The politics of Gian Galeazzo Visconti, of Louis XI of France, of Ferdinand of Spain, of the papacy, of Venice, might have been dictated by the author of *The Prince*. But Machiavelli was the first to observe, to compare, to diagnose, to analyze, and to formulate their principles of government. The first to establish, not a divorce, but rather a judicial separation between the morals of a man and the morals of a government. It is around the purpose and possible results of such a separation in politics, ethics, and religion that the storm has raged most fiercely. To follow the path of that storm through near four centuries many volumes would be needed, and it will be more convenient to deal with the more general questions in summing up the influence of Machiavelli as a whole. But the main lines and varying fortunes of the long campaign may be indicated. During the period of its manuscript circulation and for a few years after its publication *The Prince* was treated with favor or at worst with indifference, and the first mutterings were merely personal to the author. He was a scurvy knave and turncoat with neither bowels nor conscience, almost negligible. But still men read him, and a change in conditions brought a change in front. He had in *The Prince*, above all in the *Discorsi*, accused the Church of having ruined Italy and debauched the world. In view of the writer's growing popularity, of the Reformation and the Pagan Renaissance, such charges could no longer be lightly set aside. The Churchmen opened the main attack. Amongst the leaders was Cardinal Pole, to whom the practical precepts of *The Prince* had been recommended in lieu of the dreams of Plato, by Thomas Cromwell, the *malleus monachorum* of Henry VII. The Catholic attack was purely theological, but before long the Jesuits joined in the cry. Machiavelli was burnt in effigy at Ingoldstadt. He was *subdolus diabolicarum cogitatumum faber*, and *irrisor et atheos* to boot. The Pope himself gave commissions to unite against him, and his books were placed on the Index, together, it must be admitted, with those of Boccaccio, Erasmus, and Savonarola, so the company was goodly. But meanwhile, and perhaps in consequence, editions and translations of *The Prince* multiplied apace. The great figures of the world were absorbed by it. Charles V, his son, and his courtiers studied the book. Catherine de Medici brought it to France. A copy of *The Prince* was found on the murdered bodies of Henry III and Henry IV. Richelieu praised it. Sextus V analyzed it in his own handwriting. It was read at the English Court; Bacon was steeped in it, and quotes or alludes to it constantly. Hobbes and Harrington studied it.

But now another change. So then, cried Innocent Gentillet, the Huguenot, the book is a primer of despotism and Rome, and a grammar for bigots and tyrants. It doubtless is answerable for the Massacre of St. Bartholomew. The man is a *chien impur*. And in answer to this new huntsman the whole Protestant pack crashed in pursuit. Within fifty years of his death *The Prince* and Machiavelli himself had become a legend and a myth, a haunting, discomforting ghost that would not be laid. Machiavelism had grown to be a case of conscience both to Catholic and Protestant, to Theologian, Moralist, and Philosopher. In Spain the author, damned in France for his despotism and popery, was as freshly and freely damned for his civil and religious toleration. In England to the Cavaliers he was an Atheist, to the Roundheads a Jesuit. Christina of Sweden annotated him with enthusiasm. Frederick the Great published his *Anti-Machiavel* brimming with indignation, though it is impossible not to wonder what would have become of Prussia had not the Prussian king so closely followed in practice the precepts of the Florentine, above all perhaps, as Voltaire observed, in the publication of the *Anti-Machiavel* itself. No doubt in the eighteenth century, when monarchy was so firmly established as not to need Machiavelli, kings and statesmen sought to clear kingship of the supposed stain he had besmirched them with. But their reading was as little as their misunderstanding was great, and the Florentine Secretary remained the mysterious necromancer. It was left for Rousseau to describe the book of this 'honnête homme et bon citoyen' as 'le livre des Républicains,' and for Napoleon, the greatest of the author's followers if not disciples, to draw inspiration and suggestion from his Florentine forerunner and to justify the murder of the Duc d'Enghien by a quotation from *The Prince.* 'Mais après tout,' he said, 'un homme d'Etat est-il fait pour être sensible? N'est-ce pas un personnage—complètement excentrique, toujours seul d'un côté, avec le monde de l'autre?' and again 'Jugez donc s'il doit s'amuser à ménager certaines convenances de sentiments si importantes pour le commun des hommes? Peut-il considérer les liens du sang, les affections, les puérils ménagements de la société? Et dans la situation où il se trouve, que d'actions séparées de l'ensemble et qu'on blâme, quoiqu'elles doivent contribuer au grand oeuvre que tout le monde n'aperçoit pas?. . . Malheureux que vous êtes! vous retiendrez vos éloges parce que vous craindrez que le mouvement de cette grande machine ne fasse sur vous l'effet de Gulliver, qui, lorsqu'il déplaçait sa jambe, écrasait les Lilliputiens. Exhortez-vous, devancez le temps, agrandissez votre imagination, regardez de loin, et vous verrez que ces grands personnages que vous croyez violents, cruels, que sais-je? ne sont que des politiques. Ils se connaissent, se jugent mieux que vous, et, quand ils sont réellement habiles, ils savent se rendre maîtres de leurs passions car ils vont jusqu'à en calculer les effets.' Even in his carriage at Waterloo was found a French translation of *The Prince* profusely annotated.

But from the first the defense was neither idle nor weak. The assault was on the morals of the man: the fortress held for the ideas of the thinker. He does not treat of morals, therefore he is immoral, cried the plaintiff. Has he spoken truth or falsehood? Is his word the truth and will his truth prevail? was the rejoinder. In Germany and Italy especially and in France and England in less degree, philosophers and critics have argued and written without stint and without cease. As history has grown wider and more scientific so has the preponderance of opinion leaned to the Florentine's favor.

It would be impossible to recapitulate the arguments or even to indicate the varying points of view. And indeed the main hindrance in forming a just idea of *The Prince* is the constant treatment of a single side of the book and the preconceived intent of the critic. Bacon has already been mentioned. Among later names are Hobbes, Spinoza, Leibnitz. Herder gives qualified approval, while Fichte frankly throws down the glove as *The Prince*'s champion. 'Da man weiss dass politische Machtfragen nie, am wenigsten in einem verderbten Volke, mit den Mitteln der Moral zu lösen sind, so ist es unverständig das Buch von Fürsten zu verschreien. Macchiavelli hatte einen Herrscher zu schildern, keinen Klosterbruder.' The last sentence may at least be accepted as a last word by practical politicians. Ranke and Macaulay, and a host of competent Germans and Italians have lent their thought and pens to solve the riddle in the Florentine's favor. And lastly, the course of political events in Europe have seemed to many the final justification of the teaching of *The Prince*. The leaders of the Risorgimento thought that they found in letters, 'writ with a stiletto,' not only the inspirations of patriotism and the aspirations to unity, but a sure and trusted guide to the achievement. Germany recognized in the author a schoolmaster to lead them to unification, and a military instructor to teach them of an Armed People. Half Europe snatched at the principle of Nationality. For in *The Prince*, Machiavelli not only begat ideas but fertilized the ideas of others, and whatever the future estimation of the book may be, it stands, read or unread, as a most potent, if not as the dominant, factor in European politics for four hundred years.

The Discorsi, printed in Rome by Blado, 1537, are not included in the present edition, as the first English translation did not appear until 1680, when almost the entire works of Machiavelli were published by an anonymous translator in London. But some account and consideration of their contents is imperative to any review of the Florentine's political thoughts. Such *Discorsi* and Relazioni were not uncommon at the time. The stronger and younger minds of the Renaissance wearied of discussing in the lovely gardens of the Rucellai the ideas of Plato or the allegories of Plotinus. The politics of Aristotle had just been intelligibly translated by Leonardo Bruni (1492). And today the young ears and eyes of Florence were alert for an impulse to action. They saw glimpses, in reopened fields of history, of quarries long grown over where the ore of positive politics lay hid. The men who came today to the Orti Oricellarii were men versed in public affairs, men of letters, historians, poets, living greatly in a great age, with Raphael, Michael Angelo, Ariosto, Leonardo going up and down amongst them. Machiavelli was now in fair favor with the Medici, and is described by Strozzi as *una persona per sorgere* (a rising man). He was welcomed into the group with enthusiasm, and there read and discussed the *Discorsi*. Nominally mere considerations upon the First Decade of Livy, they rapidly encircled all that was known and thought of policy and statecraft, old and living.

Written concurrently with *The Prince*, though completed later, the *Discorsi* contain almost the whole of the thoughts and intents of the more famous book, but with a slightly different application. '*The Prince* traces the progress of an ambitious man, the *Discorsi* the progress of an ambitious people,' is an apt if inadequate criticism. Machiavelli was not the first Italian who thought and wrote upon the problems of his time. But he was the first who discussed grave questions in modern language. He was the first modern political writer who wrote of men and not of man, for the Prince himself is a collective individuality. 'This must be regarded as a general rule,' is ever in Machiavelli's mouth, while Guicciardini finds no value in a general rule, but only in 'long experience and worthy discretion.' The one treated of policy, the other of politics. Guicciardini considered specifically by what methods to control and arrange an existing Government. Machiavelli sought to create a science, which should show how to establish, maintain, and hinder the decline of states generally conceived. Even Cavour counted the former as a more practical guide in affairs. But Machiavelli was the theorist of humanity in politics, not the observer only. He distinguished the two orders of research. And, during the Italian Renaissance such distinction was supremely necessary. With a crumbled theology, a pagan Pope, amid the wreck of laws and the confusion of social order, *il suo particolare* and *virtù*, individuality and ability (energy, political genius, prowess, vital force: *virtù* is impossible to translate, and only does not mean virtue), were the dominating and unrelenting factors of life. Niccolò Machiavelli, unlike Montesquieu, agreed with Martin Luther that man was bad. It was for both the Wittenberger and the Florentine, in their very separate ways, to found the school and wield the scourge. In the naked and unashamed candor of the time Guicciardini could say that he loathed the Papacy and all its works. 'For all that,' he adds, 'the preferments I have enjoyed, have forced me for my private ends to set my heart upon papal greatness. Were it not for this consideration, I should love Martin Luther as my second self.' In the *Discorsi*, Machiavelli bitterly arraigns the Church as having 'deprived Italians of religion and liberty.' He utterly condemns Savonarola; yet he could love and learn from Dante, and might almost have said with Pym, 'The greatest liberty of the Kingdom is Religion. Thereby we are freed from spiritual evils, and no impositions are so grievous as those that are laid upon the soul.'

The Florentine postulates religion as an essential element in a strong and stable State. Perhaps, with Gibbon, he deemed it useful to the Magistrate. But his science is impersonal. He will not tolerate a Church that poaches on his political preserves. Good dogma makes bad politics. It must not tamper with liberty or security. And most certainly, with Dante, in the *Paradiso*, he would either have transformed or omitted the third Beatitude, that the Meek shall inherit the earth. With such a temperament, Machiavelli must ever keep touch with sanity. It was not for him as for Aristotle to imagine what an ideal State should be, but rather to inquire what States actually were and what they might actually become. He seeks first and foremost the use that may be derived 'from history in politics'; not from its incidents but from its general principles. His darling model of a State is to be found where Dante found it, in the Roman Republic. The memory and even the substance of Dante occur again and again. But Dante's inspiration was spiritual: Machiavelli's frankly pagan, and with the latter Fortune takes the place of God. Dante did not love the Papacy, but Machiavelli, pointing out how even in ancient Rome religion was politic or utilitarian, leads up to his famous attack upon the Roman Church, to which he attributes all the shame and losses, political, social, moral, national, that Italy has suffered at her hands. And now for the first time the necessity for Italian Unity is laid plainly down, and the Church and its temporal power denounced as the central obstacles. In religion itself the Secretary saw much merit.['But when it is an absolute question of the welfare of our country, then justice or injustice, mercy or cruelty, praise or ignominy, must be set aside, and we must seek alone whatever course may preserve the existence and liberty of the state.']Throughout the *Discorsi*, Machiavelli in a looser and more expansive form, suggests, discusses, or reaffirms the ideas of *The Prince*. There is the same absence of judgment on the moral value of individual conduct; the same keen decision of its practical effect as a political act. But here more than in *The Prince*, he deals with the action and conduct of the people. With his passion for personal and contemporary incarnation he finds in the Swiss of his day the Romans of Republican Rome, and reiterates the comparison in detail. Feudalism, mercenaries, political associations embodied in Arts and Guilds, the Temporal power of the Church, all these are put away, and in their stead he announces the new and daring gospel that for organic unity subjects must be treated as equals and not as inferiors. 'Trust the people' is a maxim he repeats and enforces again and again. And he does not shrink from, but rather urges the corollary, 'Arm the people.' Indeed it were no audacious paradox to state the ideal of Machiavelli, though he nominally preferred a Republic, as a Limited Monarchy, ruling over a Nation in Arms. No doubt he sought, as was natural enough in his day, to construct the State from without rather than to guide and encourage its evolution from within. It seemed to him that, in such an ocean of corruption, Force *was* a remedy and Fraud no sluttish handmaid. 'Vice n'est-ce pas,' writes Montaigne, of such violent acts of Government, 'car il a quitté sa raison à une plus universelle et puissante raison.' Even so the Prince and the people could only be justified by results. But the public life is of larger value than the private, and sometimes one man must be crucified for a thousand. Despite all prejudice and make-belief, such a rule and practice has obtained from the Assemblies of Athens to the Parliaments of the twentieth century. But Machiavelli first candidly imparted it to the unwilling consciences and brains of men, and it is he who has been the chosen scapegoat to carry the sins of the people. His earnestness makes him belie his own precept to keep the name and take away the thing. In this, as in a thousand instances, he was not too darkly hidden; he was too plain. 'Machiavelli,' says one who studied the Florentine as hardly another had done, 'Machiavelli hat gesündigt, aber noch mehr ist gegen ihn gesündigt worden.' Liberty is good, but Unity is its only sure foundation. It is the way to the Unity of Government and People that the thoughts both of *The Prince* and the *Discorsi* lead, though the incidents be so nakedly presented as to shock the timorous and vex the prurient, the puritan, and the evil thinker. The people must obey the State and fight and die for its salvation, and for the Prince the hatred of the subjects is never good, but their love, and the best way to gain it is by 'not interrupting the subject in the quiet enjoyment of his estate.' Even so bland and gentle a spirit as the poet Gray cannot but comment, 'I rejoice when I see Machiavelli defended or illustrated, who to me appears one of the wisest men that any nation in any age hath produced.'

Throughout both *The Prince* and the *Discorsi* are constant allusions to, and often long discussions on, military affairs. The Army profoundly interested Machiavelli both as a primary condition of national existence and stability, and also, as he pondered upon the contrast between ancient Rome and the Florence that he lived in, as a subject fascinating in itself. His *Art of War* was probably published in 1520. Before that date the Florentine Secretary had had some personal touch both with the theory and practice of war. As a responsible official in the camp before Pisa he had seen both siege work and fighting. Having lost faith in mercenary forces he made immense attempts to form a National Militia, and was appointed Chancellor of the Nove della Milizia. In Switzerland and the Tyrol he had studied army questions. He planned with Pietro Navarro the defense of Florence and Prato against Charles V. At Verona and Mantua in 1509, he closely studied the famous siege of Padua. From birth to death, war and battles raged all about him, and he had personal knowledge of the great captains of the Age. Moreover, he saw in Italy troops of every country, of every quality, in every stage of discipline, in every manner of formation. His love of ancient Rome led him naturally to the study of Livy and Vegetius, and from them with regard to formations, to the relative values of infantry and cavalry and other points of tactics, he drew or deduced many conclusions which hold good today. Indeed a German staff officer has written that in reading the Florentine you think you are listening to a modern theorist of war. But for the theorist of those days a lion stood in the path. The art of war was not excepted from the quick and thorough transformation that all earthly and spiritual things were undergoing. Gunpowder, long invented, was being applied. Armor, that, since the beginning, had saved both man and horse, had now lost the half of its virtue. The walls of fortresses, impregnable for a thousand years, became as matchwood ramparts. The mounted man-at-arms was found with wonder to be no match for the lightly-armored but nimble foot-man. The Swiss were seen to hold their own with ease against the knighthood of Austria and Burgundy. The Free Companies lost in value and prestige what they added to their corruption and treachery. All these things grew clear to Machiavelli. But his almost fatal misfortune was that he observed and wrote in the mid-moment of the transition. He had no faith in fire-arms, and as regards the portable fire-arms of those days he was right. After the artillery work at Ravenna, Novara, and Marignano it is argued that he should have known better. But he was present at no great battles, and pike, spear, and sword had been the stable weapons of four thousand years. These were indeed too simple to be largely modified, and the future of mechanisms and explosives no prophet uninspired could foresee. And indeed the armament and formation of men were not the main intent of Machiavelli's thought. His care in detail, especially in fortifications, of which he made a special study, in encampments, in plans, in calculations, is immense. Nothing is so trivial as to be left inexact.

But he centred his observation and imagination on the origin, character, and discipline of an army in being. He pictures the horror, waste, and failure of a mercenary system, and lays down the fatal error in Italy of separating civil from military life, converting the latter into a trade. In such a way the soldier grows to a beast, and the citizen to a coward. All this must be changed. The basic idea of this astounding Secretary is to form a National Army, furnished by conscription and informed by the spirit of the New Model of Cromwell. All able-bodied men between the ages of seventeen and forty should be drilled on stated days and be kept in constant readiness. Once or twice a year each battalion must be mobilized and maneuvered as in time of war. The discipline must be constant and severe. The men must be not only robust and well-trained, but, above all, virtuous, modest, and disposed to any sacrifice for the public good. So imbued should they be with duty and lofty devotion to their country that though they may rightly deceive the enemy, reward the enemy's deserters and employ spies, yet 'an apple tree laden with fruit might stand untouched in the midst of their encampment.' The infantry should far exceed the cavalry, 'since it is by infantry that battles are won.' Secrecy, mobility, and familiarity with the country are to be objects of special care, and positions should be chosen from which advance is safer than retreat. In war this army must be led by one single leader, and, when peace shines again, they must go back contented to their grateful fellow-countrymen and their wonted ways of living. The conception and foundation of such a scheme, at such a time, by such a man is indeed astounding. He broke with the past and with all contemporary organizations. He forecast the future of military Europe, though his own Italy was the last to win her redemption through his plans. 'Taken all in all,' says a German military writer, 'we may recognize Machiavelli in his inspired knowledge of the principles of universal military discipline as a true prophet, and as one of the weightiest thinkers in the field of military construction and constitution. He penetrated the essence of military technique with a precision wholly alien to his period, and it is, so to say, a new psychological proof of the relationship between the art of war and the art of statecraft, that the founder of Modern Politics is also the first of modern Military Classics.'

But woe to the Florentine Secretary with his thoughts born centuries before their time. As in *The Prince*, so in the *Art of War*, he closes with a passionate appeal of great sorrow and the smallest ray of hope. Where shall I hope to find the things that I have told of? What is Italy today? What are the Italians? Enervated, impotent, vile. Wherefore, 'I lament me of nature, the which either ought not to have made me a knower of this, or it ought to have given me power, to have bene able to have executed it: For now being old, I cannot hope to have any occasion, to be able so to do: In consideration whereof, I have been liberal with you who being grave young men, may (when the things said of me shall please you) at due times, in favor of your Princes, help them and consider them. Wherein I would have you not to be afraid, or mistrustful, because this Province seems to be altogether given to raise up again the things dead, as is seen by the perfection that Poesy, painting, and writing, is now brought unto: Albeit, as much as is looked for of me, being stricken in years, I do mistrust. Where surely, if Fortune had heretofore granted me so much state, as sufficeth for a like enterprise, I would not have doubted, but in most short time, to have showed to the world, how much the ancient orders avail: and without peradventure, either I would have increased it with glory, or lost it without shame.'

In 1520 Machiavelli was an ageing and disappointed of man. He was not popular with any party, but the Medici were willing to use him in minor matters if only to secure his adherence. He was commissioned by Giulio de Medici to write a history of Florence with an annual allowance of 100 florins. In 1525 he completed his task and dedicated the book to its begetter, Pope Clement VII.

In the History, as in much of his other work, Machiavelli enriches the science of humanity with a new department. 'He was the first to contemplate the life of a nation in its continuity, to trace the operation of political forces through successive generations, to contrast the action of individuals with the evolution of causes over which they had but little control, and to bring the salient features of the national biography into relief by the suppression of comparatively unimportant details.' He found no examples to follow, for Villani with all his merits was of a different order. Diarists and chroniclers there were in plenty, and works of the learned men led by Aretino, written in Latin and mainly rhetorical. The great work of Guicciardini was not published till years after the Secretary's death. Machiavelli broke away from the Chronicle or any other existing form. He deliberately applied philosophy to the sequence of facts. He organized civil and political history. He originally intended to begin his work at the year 1234, the year of the return of Cosimo il Vecchio from exile and of the consolidation of Medicean power on the ground that the earlier periods had been covered by Aretino and Bracciolini. But he speedily recognized that they told of nothing but external wars and business while the heart of the history of Florence was left unbared. The work was to do again in very different manner, and in that manner he did it. Throughout he maintains and insistently insinuates his unfailing explanation of the miseries of Italy; the necessity of unity and the evils of the Papacy which prevents it. In this book dedicated to a Pope he scants nothing of his hatred of the Holy See. For ever he is still seeking the one strong man in a blatant land with almost absolute power to punish, pull down, and reconstruct on an abiding foundation, for to his clear eyes it is ever the events that are born of the man, and not the man of the events. He was the first to observe that the Ghibellines were not only the Imperial party but the party of the aristocrats and influential men, whereas the Guelphs were the party not only of the Church but of the people, and he traces the slow but increasing struggle to the triumph of democracy in the Ordinamenti di Giustizia (1293). But the triumph was not final. The Florentines were 'unable to preserve liberty and could not tolerate slavery.' So the fighting, banishments, bloodshed, cruelty, injustice, began once more. The nobles were in origin Germanic, he points out, the people Latin; so that a racial bitterness gave accent to their hate. But yet, he adds impartially, when the crushed nobility were forced to change their names and no longer dared be heard, 'Florence was not only stripped of arms but likewise of all generosity.' It would be impossible to follow the History in detail. The second, seventh and eighth books are perhaps the most powerful and dramatic. Outside affairs and lesser events are lightly touched. But no stories in the world have been told with more intensity than those of the conspiracies in the seventh and eighth books, and none have given a more intimate and accurate perception of the modes of thought and feeling at the time. The History ends with the death of Lorenzo de Medici in 1492. Enough has been said of its breadth of scope and originality of method. The spirit of clear flaming patriotism, of undying hope that will not in the darkest day despair, the plangent appeal to Italy for its own great sake to rouse and live, all these are found preeminently in the History as they are found wherever Machiavelli speaks from the heart of his heart. Of the style a foreigner may not speak. But those who are proper judges maintain that in simplicity and lucidity, vigor, and power, softness, elevation, and eloquence, the style of Machiavelli is 'divine,' and remains, as that of Dante among the poets, unchallenged and insuperable among all writers of Italian prose.

Though Machiavelli must always stand as a political thinker, an historian, and a military theorist it would leave an insufficient idea of his mental activities were there no short notice of his other literary works. With his passion for incarnating his theories in a single personality, he wrote the *Life of Castruccio Castracani*, a politico-military romance. His hero was a soldier of fortune born at Lucca in 1281, and, playing with a free hand, Machiavelli weaves a life of adventure and romance in which his constant ideas of war and politics run through and across an almost imaginary tapestry. He seems to have intended to illustrate and to popularize his ideals and to attain by a story the many whom his discourses could not reach. In verse Machiavelli was fluent, pungent, and prosaic. The unfinished *Golden Ass* is merely made of paragraphs of the *Discorsi* twined into rhymes. And the others are little better. Countless pamphlets, essays, and descriptions may be searched without total waste by the very curious and the very leisurely. The many despatches and multitudinous private letters tell the story both of his life and his mind. But the short but famous *Novella di Belfagor Arcidiavolo* is excellent in wit, satire, and invention. As a playwright he wrote, among many lesser efforts, one supreme comedy, *Mandragola*, which Macaulay declares to be better than the best of Goldoni's plays, and only less excellent than the very best of Moliere's. Italian critics call it the finest play in Italian. The plot is not for nursery reading, but there are tears and laughter and pity and anger to furnish forth a copious author, and it has been not ill observed that *Mandragola* is the comedy of a society of which *The Prince* is the tragedy.

It has been said of the Italians of the Renaissance that with so much of unfairness in their policy, there was an extraordinary degree of fairness in their intellects. They were as direct in thought as they were tortuous in action, and could see no wickedness in deceiving a man whom they intended to destroy. To such a charge—if charge it be— Machiavelli would have willingly owned himself answerable. He observed, in order to know, and he wished to use his knowledge for the advancement of good. To him the means were indifferent, provided only that they were always apt and moderate in accordance with necessity. A surgeon has no room for sentiment: in such an operator pity were a crime. It is his to examine, to probe, to diagnose, flinching at no ulcer, sparing neither to himself or to his patient. And if he may not act, he is to lay down very clearly the reasons which led to his conclusions and to state the mode by which life itself may be saved, cost what amputation and agony it may. This was Machiavelli's business, and he applied his eye, his brains, and his knife with a relentless persistence, which, only because it was so faithful, was not called heroic. And we know that he suffered in the doing of it and that his heart was sore for his patient. But there was no other way. His record is clear and shining. He has been accused of no treachery, of no evil action. His patriotism for Italy as a fatherland, a dream undreamt by any other, never glowed more brightly than when Italy lay low in shame, and ruin, and despair. His faith never faltered, his spirit never shrank. And the Italy that he saw, through dark bursts of storm, broken and sinking, we see today riding in the sunny haven where he would have her to be.

HENRY CUST

1905.

Dedication

TO THE MAGNIFICENT LORENZO DI PIERO DE' MEDICI

It is customary for such as seek a Prince's favour, to present themselves before him with those things of theirs which they themselves most value, or in which they perceive him chiefly to delight. Accordingly, we often see horses, armour, cloth of gold, precious stones, and the like costly gifts, offered to Princes as worthy of their greatness. Desiring in like manner to approach your Magnificence with some token of my devotion, I have found among my possessions none that I so much prize and esteem as a knowledge of the actions of great men, acquired in the course of a long experience of modern affairs and a continual study of antiquity. Which knowledge most carefully and patiently pondered over and sifted by me, and now reduced into this little book, I send to your Magnificence. And though I deem the work unworthy of your greatness, yet am I bold enough to hope that your courtesy will dispose you to accept it, considering that I can offer you no better gift than the means of mastering in a very brief time, all that in the course of so many years, and at the cost of so many hardships and dangers, I have learned, and know.

This work I have not adorned or amplified with rounded periods, swelling and high-flown language, or any other of those extrinsic attractions and allurements wherewith many authors are wont to set off and grace their writings; since it is my desire that it should either pass wholly unhonoured, or that the truth of its matter and the importance of its subject should alone recommend it.

Nor would I have it thought presumption that a person of very mean and humble station should venture to discourse and lay down rules concerning the government of Princes. For as those who make maps of countries place themselves low down in the plains to study the character of mountains and elevated lands, and place themselves high up on the mountains to get a better view of the plains, so in like manner to understand the People a man should be a Prince, and to have a clear notion of Princes he should belong to the People.

Let your Magnificence, then, accept this little gift in the spirit in which I offer it; wherein, if you diligently read and study it, you will recognize my extreme desire that you should attain to that eminence which Fortune and your own merits promise you. Should you from the height of your greatness some time turn your eyes to these humble regions, you will become aware how undeservedly I have to endure the keen and unremitting malignity of Fortune.

NICCOLÒ MACHIAVELLI

Chapter I.

Of the Various Kinds of Princedom, and of the Ways
in Which They Are Acquired

All the States and Governments by which men are or ever have been ruled, have been and are either Republics or Princedoms. Princedoms are either hereditary, in which the sovereignty is derived through an ancient line of ancestors, or they are new. New Princedoms are either wholly new, as that of Milan to Francesco Sforza; or they are like limbs joined on to the hereditary possessions of the Prince who acquires them, as the Kingdom of Naples to the dominions of the King of Spain. The States thus acquired have either been used to live under a Prince or have been free; and he who acquires them does so either by his own arms or by the arms of others, and either by good fortune or by merit.

Chapter II.

Of Hereditary Princedoms

Of Republics I shall not now speak, having elsewhere spoken of them at length. Here I shall treat exclusively of Princedoms, and, filling in the outline above traced out, shall proceed to examine how such States are to be governed and maintained.

I say, then, that hereditary States, accustomed to the family of their Prince, are maintained with far less difficulty than new States, since all that is required is that the Prince shall not depart from the usages of his ancestors, trusting for the rest to deal with events as they arise. So that if an hereditary Prince be of average address, he will always maintain himself in his Princedom, unless deprived of it by some extraordinary and irresistible force; and even if so deprived will recover it, should any, even the least, mishap overtake the usurper. We have in Italy an example of this in the Duke of Ferrara, who never could have withstood the attacks of the Venetians in 1484, nor those of Pope Julius in 1510, had not his authority in that State been consolidated by time. For since a Prince by birth has fewer occasions and less need to give offence, he ought to be better loved, and will naturally be popular with his subjects unless outrageous vices make him odious. Moreover, the very antiquity and continuance of his rule will efface the memories and causes which lead to innovation. For one change always leaves a dovetail into which another will fit.

Chapter III.

Of Mixed Princedoms

But in new Princedoms difficulties abound. And, first, if the Princedom be not wholly new, but joined on to the ancient dominions of the Prince, so as to form with them what may be termed a mixed Princedom, changes will come from a cause common to all new States, namely, that men, thinking to better their condition, are always ready to change masters, and in this expectation will take up arms against any ruler; wherein they deceive themselves, and find afterwards by experience that they are worse off than before. This again results naturally and necessarily from the circumstance that the Prince cannot avoid giving offence to his new subjects, either in respect of the troops he quarters on them, or of some other of the numberless vexations attendant on a new acquisition. And in this way you may find that you have enemies in all those whom you have injured in seizing the Princedom, yet cannot keep the friendship of those who helped you to gain it; since you can neither reward them as they expect, nor yet, being under obligations to them, use violent remedies against them. For however strong you may be in respect of your army, it is essential that in entering a new Province you should have the good will of its inhabitants.

Hence it happened that Louis XII of France, speedily gaining possession of Milan, as speedily lost it; and that on the occasion of its first capture, Lodovico Sforza was able with his own forces only to take it from him. For the very people who had opened the gates to the French King, when they found themselves deceived in their expectations and hopes of future benefits, could not put up with the insolence of their new ruler. True it is that when a State rebels and is again got under, it will not afterwards be lost so easily. For the Prince, using the rebellion as a pretext, will not scruple to secure himself by punishing the guilty, bringing the suspected to trial, and otherwise strengthening his position in the points where it was weak. So that if to recover Milan from the French it was enough on the first occasion that a Duke Lodovico should raise alarms on the frontiers to wrest it from them a second time the whole world had to be ranged against them, and their armies destroyed and driven out of Italy. And this for the reasons above assigned. And yet, for a second time, Milan was lost to the King. The general causes of its first loss have been shown. It remains to note the causes of the second, and to point out the remedies which the French King had, or which might have been used by another in like circumstances to maintain his conquest more successfully than he did.

I say, then, that those States which upon their acquisition are joined on to the ancient dominions of the Prince who acquires them, are either of the same Province and tongue as the people of these dominions, or they are not. When they are, there is a great ease in retaining them, especially when they have not been accustomed to live in freedom. To hold them securely it is enough to have rooted out the line of the reigning Prince; because if in other respects the old condition of things be continued, and there be no discordance in their customs, men live peaceably with one another, as we see to have been the case in Brittany, Burgundy, Gascony, and Normandy, which have so long been united to France. For although there be some slight difference in their languages, their customs are similar, and they can easily get on together. He, therefore, who acquires such a State, if he mean to keep it, must see to two things; first, that the blood of the ancient line of Princes be destroyed; second, that no change be made in respect of laws or taxes; for in this way the newly acquired State speedily becomes incorporated with the hereditary.

But when States are acquired in a country differing in language, usages, and laws, difficulties multiply, and great good fortune, as well as address, is needed to overcome them. One of the best and most efficacious methods for dealing with such a State, is for the Prince who acquires it to go and dwell there in person, since this will tend to make his tenure more secure and lasting. This course has been followed by the Turk with regard to Greece, who, had he not, in addition to all his other precautions for securing that Province, himself come to live in it, could never have kept his hold of it. For when you are on the spot, disorders are detected in their beginnings and remedies can be readily applied; but when you are at a distance, they are not heard of until they have gathered strength and the case is past cure. Moreover, the Province in which you take up your abode is not pillaged by your officers; the people are pleased to have a ready recourse to their Prince; and have all the more reason if they are well disposed, to love, if disaffected, to fear him. A foreign enemy desiring to attack that State would be cautious how he did so. In short, where the Prince resides in person, it will be extremely difficult to oust him.

Another excellent expedient is to send colonies into one or two places, so that these may become, as it were, the keys of the Province; for you must either do this, or else keep up a numerous force of men-at-arms and foot soldiers. A Prince need not spend much on colonies. He can send them out and support them at little or no charge to himself, and the only persons to whom he gives offence are those whom he deprives of their fields and houses to bestow them on the new inhabitants. Those who are thus injured form but a small part of the community, and remaining scattered and poor can never become dangerous. All others being left unmolested, are in consequence easily quieted, and at the same time are afraid to make a false move, lest they share the fate of those who have been deprived of their possessions. In few words, these colonies cost less than soldiers, are more faithful, and give less offence, while those who are offended, being, as I have said, poor and dispersed, cannot hurt. And let it here be noted that men are either to be kindly treated, or utterly crushed, since they can revenge lighter injuries, but not graver. Wherefore the injury we do to a man should be of a sort to leave no fear of reprisals.

But if instead of colonies you send troops, the cost is vastly greater, and the whole revenues of the country are spent in guarding it; so that the gain becomes a loss, and much deeper offence is given; since in shifting the quarters of your soldiers from place to place the whole country suffers hardship, which as all feel, all are made enemies; and enemies who remaining, although vanquished, in their own homes, have power to hurt. In every way, therefore, this mode of defence is as disadvantageous as that by colonizing is useful.

The Prince who establishes himself in a Province whose laws and language differ from those of his own people, ought also to make himself the head and protector of his feebler neighbours, and endeavour to weaken the stronger, and must see that by no accident shall any other stranger as powerful as himself find an entrance there. For it will always happen that some such person will be called in by those of the Province who are discontented either through ambition or fear; as we see of old the Romans brought into Greece by the Aetolians, and in every other country that they entered, invited there by its inhabitants. And the usual course of things is that so soon as a formidable stranger enters a Province, all the weaker powers side with him, moved thereto by the ill-will they bear towards him who has hitherto kept them in subjection. So that in respect of these lesser powers, no trouble is needed to gain them over, for at once, together, and of their own accord, they throw in their lot with the government of the stranger. The new Prince, therefore, has only to see that they do not increase too much in strength, and with his own forces, aided by their good will, can easily subdue any who are powerful, so as to remain supreme in the Province. He who does not manage this matter well, will soon lose whatever he has gained, and while he retains it will find in it endless troubles and annoyances.

In dealing with the countries of which they took possession the Romans diligently followed the methods I have described. They planted colonies, conciliated weaker powers without adding to their strength, humbled the great, and never suffered a formidable stranger to acquire influence. A single example will suffice to show this. In Greece the Romans took the Achaians and Aetolians into their pay; the Macedonian monarchy was humbled; Antiochus was driven out. But the services of the Achaians and Aetolians never obtained for them any addition to their power; no persuasions on the part of Philip could induce the Romans to be his friends on the condition of sparing him humiliation; nor could all the power of Antiochus bring them to consent to his exercising any authority within that Province. And in thus acting the Romans did as all wise rulers should, who have to consider not only present difficulties but also future, against which they must use all diligence to provide; for these, if they be foreseen while yet remote, admit of easy remedy, but if their approach be awaited, are already past cure, the disorder having become hopeless; realizing what the physicians tell us of hectic fever, that in its beginning it is easy to cure, but hard to recognize; whereas, after a time, not having been detected and treated at the first, it becomes easy to recognize but impossible to cure.

And so it is with State affairs. For the distempers of a State being discovered while yet inchoate, which can only be done by a sagacious ruler, may easily be dealt with; but when, from not being observed, they are suffered to grow until they are obvious to everyone, there is no longer any remedy. The Romans, therefore, foreseeing evils while they were yet far off, always provided against them, and never suffered them to take their course for the sake of avoiding war; since they knew that war is not so to be avoided, but is only postponed to the advantage of the other side. They chose, therefore, to make war with Philip and Antiochus in Greece, that they might not have to make it with them in Italy, although for a while they might have escaped both. This they did not desire, nor did the maxim *leave it to Time*, which the wise men of our own day have always on their lips, ever recommend itself to them. What they looked to enjoy were the fruits of their own valour and foresight. For Time, driving all things before it, may bring with it evil as well as good.

But let us now go back to France and examine whether she has followed any of those methods of which I have made mention. I shall speak of Louis and not of Charles, because from the former having held longer possession of Italy, his manner of acting is more plainly seen. You will find, then, that he has done the direct opposite of what he should have done in order to retain a foreign State.

King Louis was brought into Italy by the ambition of the Venetians, who hoped by his coming to gain for themselves a half of the State of Lombardy. I will not blame this coming, nor the part taken by the King, because, desiring to gain a footing in Italy, where he had no friends, but on the contrary, owing to the conduct of Charles, every door was shut against him, he was driven to accept such friendships as he could get. And his designs might easily have succeeded had he not made mistakes in other particulars of conduct.

By the recovery of Lombardy, Louis at once regained the credit which Charles had lost. Genoa made submission; the Florentines came to terms; the Marquis of Mantua, the Duke of Ferrara, the Bentivogli, the Countess of Forli, the Lords of Faenza, Pesaro, Rimini, Camerino, and Piombino, the citizens of Lucca, Pisa, and Siena, all came forward offering their friendship. The Venetians, who to obtain possession of a couple of towns in Lombardy had made the French King master of two-thirds of Italy, had now cause to repent the rash game they had played.

Let anyone, therefore, consider how easily King Louis might have maintained his authority in Italy had he observed the rules which I have noted above, and secured and protected all those friends of his, who being weak, and fearful, some of the Church, some of the Venetians, were of necessity obliged to attach themselves to him, and with whose assistance, for they were many, he might readily have made himself safe against any other powerful State. But no sooner was he in Milan than he took a contrary course, in helping Pope Alexander to occupy Romagna; not perceiving that in seconding this enterprise he weakened himself by alienating friends and those who had thrown themselves into his arms, while he strengthened the Church by adding great temporal power to the spiritual power which of itself confers so mighty an authority. Making this first mistake, he was forced to follow it up, until at last, in order to curb the ambition of Pope Alexander, and prevent him becoming master of Tuscany, he was obliged to come himself into Italy.

And as though it were not enough for him to have aggrandized the Church and stripped himself of friends, he must needs in his desire to possess the Kingdom of Naples, divide it with the King of Spain; thus bringing into Italy, where before he had been supreme, a rival to whom the ambitious and discontented in that Province might have recourse. And whereas he might have left in Naples a King willing to hold as his tributary, he displaced him to make way for another strong enough to effect his expulsion. The wish to acquire is no doubt a natural and common sentiment, and when men attempt things within their power, they will always be praised rather than blamed. But when they persist in attempts that are beyond their power, mishaps and blame ensue. If France, therefore, with her own forces could have attacked Naples, she should have done so. If she could not, she ought not to have divided it. And if her partition of Lombardy with the Venetians may be excused as the means whereby a footing was gained in Italy, this other partition is to be condemned as not justified by the like necessity.

Louis, then, had made these five blunders. He had destroyed weaker States, he had strengthened a Prince already strong, he had brought into the country a very powerful stranger, he had not come to reside, and he had not sent colonies. And yet all these blunders might not have proved disastrous to him while he lived, had he not added to them a sixth in depriving the Venetians of their dominions. For had he neither aggrandized the Church, nor brought Spain into Italy, it might have been at once reasonable and necessary to humble the Venetians; but after committing himself to these other courses, he should never have consented to the ruin of Venice. For while the Venetians were powerful they would always have kept others back from an attempt on Lombardy, as well because they never would have agreed to that enterprise on any terms save of themselves being made its masters, as because others would never have desired to take it from France in order to hand it over to them, nor would ever have ventured to defy both. And if it be said that King Louis ceded Romagna to Alexander, and Naples to Spain in order to avoid war, I answer that for the reasons already given, you ought never to suffer your designs to be crossed in order to avoid war, since war is not so to be avoided, but is only deferred to your disadvantage. And if others should allege the King's promise to the Pope to undertake that enterprise on his behalf, in return for the dissolution of his marriage, and for the Cardinal's hat conferred on d'Amboise, I answer by referring to what I say further on concerning the faith of Princes and how it is to be kept.

King Louis, therefore, lost Lombardy from not following any one of the methods pursued by others who have taken Provinces with the resolve to keep them. Nor is this anything strange, but only what might reasonably and naturally be looked for. And on this very subject I spoke to d'Amboise at Nantes, at the time when Duke Valentino, as Cesare Borgia, son to Pope Alexander, was vulgarly called, was occupying Romagna. For, on the Cardinal saying to me that the Italians did not understand war, I answered that the French did not understand statecraft, for had they done so, they never would have allowed the Church to grow so powerful. And the event shows that the aggrandizement of the Church and of Spain in Italy has been brought about by France, and that the ruin of France has been wrought by them. Whence we may draw the general axiom, which never or rarely errs, that *he who is the cause of another's greatness is himself undone*, since he must work either by address or force, each of which excites distrust in the person raised to power.

Chapter IV.

Why the Kingdom of Darius, Conquered by Alexander, Did Not, on Alexander's Death, Rebel Against His Successors

Alexander the Great having achieved the conquest of Asia in a few years, and dying before he had well entered on possession, it might have been expected, having regard to the difficulty of preserving newly acquired States, that on his death the whole country would rise in revolt. Nevertheless, his successors were able to keep their hold, and found in doing so no other difficulty than arose from their own ambition and mutual jealousies.

If anyone think this strange and ask the cause, I answer, that all the Princedoms of which we have record have been governed in one or other of two ways, either by a sole Prince, all others being his servants permitted by his grace and favour to assist in governing the kingdom as his ministers; or else, by a Prince with his Barons who hold their rank, not by the favour of a superior Lord, but by antiquity of blood, and who have States and subjects of their own who recognize them as their rulers and entertain for them a natural affection. States governed by a sole Prince and by his servants vest in him a more complete authority; because throughout the land none but he is recognized as sovereign, and if obedience be yielded to any others, it is yielded as to his ministers and officers for whom personally no special love is felt.

Of these two forms of government we have examples in our own days in the Turk and the King of France. The whole Turkish empire is governed by a sole Prince, all others being his slaves. Dividing his kingdom into *sandjaks*, he sends thither different governors whom he shifts and changes at his pleasure. The King of France, on the other hand, is surrounded by a multitude of nobles of ancient descent, each acknowledged and loved by subjects of his own, and each asserting a precedence in rank of which the King can deprive him only at his peril.

He, therefore, who considers the different character of these two States, will perceive that it would be difficult to gain possession of that of the Turk, but that once won it might be easily held. The obstacles to its conquest are that the invader cannot be called in by a native nobility, nor expect his enterprise to be aided by the defection of those whom the sovereign has around him. And this for the various reasons already given, namely, that all being slaves and under obligations they are not easily corrupted, or if corrupted can render little assistance, being unable, as I have already explained, to carry the people with them. Whoever, therefore, attacks the Turk must reckon on finding a united people, and must trust rather to his own strength than to divisions on the other side. But were his adversary once overcome and defeated in the field, so that he could not repair his armies, no cause for anxiety would remain, except in the family of the Prince; which being extirpated, there would be none else to fear; for since all beside are without credit with the people, the invader, as before his victory he had nothing to hope from them, so after it has nothing to dread.

But the contrary is the case in kingdoms governed like that of France, into which, because men who are discontented and desirous of change are always to be found, you may readily procure an entrance by gaining over some Baron of the Realm. Such persons, for the reasons already given, are able to open the way to you for the invasion of their country and to render its conquest easy. But afterwards the effort to hold your ground involves you in endless difficulties, as well in respect of those who have helped you, as of those whom you have overthrown. Nor will it be enough to have destroyed the family of the Prince, since all those other Lords remain to put themselves at the head of new movements; whom being unable either to content or to destroy, you lose the State whenever occasion serves them.

Now, if you examine the nature of the government of Darius, you will find that it resembled that of the Turk, and, consequently, that it was necessary for Alexander, first of all, to defeat him utterly and strip him of his dominions; after which defeat, Darius having died, the country, for the causes above explained, was permanently secured to Alexander. And had his successors continued united they might have enjoyed it undisturbed, since there arose no disorders in that kingdom save those of their own creating.

But kingdoms ordered like that of France cannot be retained with the same ease. Hence the repeated risings of Spain, Gaul, and Greece against the Romans, resulting from the number of small Princedoms of which these Provinces were made up. For while the memory of these lasted, the Romans could never think their tenure safe. But when that memory was worn out by the authority and long continuance of their rule, they gained a secure hold, and were able afterwards in their contests among themselves, each to carry with him some portion of these Provinces, according as each had acquired influence there; for these, on the extinction of the line of their old Princes, came to recognize no other Lords than the Romans.

Bearing all this in mind, no one need wonder at the ease wherewith Alexander was able to lay a firm hold on Asia, nor that Pyrrhus and many others found difficulty in preserving other acquisitions; since this arose, not from the less or greater merit of the conquerors, but from the different character of the States with which they had to deal.

Chapter V.

How Cities or Provinces Which Before Their Acquisition Have Lived Under Their Own Laws Are To Be Governed

When a newly acquired State has been accustomed, as I have said, to live under its own laws and in freedom, there are three methods whereby it may be held. The first is to destroy it; the second, to go and reside there in person; the third, to suffer it to live on under its own laws, subjecting it to a tribute, and entrusting its government to a few of the inhabitants who will keep the rest your friends. Such a Government, since it is the creature of the new Prince, will see that it cannot stand without his protection and support, and must therefore do all it can to maintain him; and a city accustomed to live in freedom, if it is to be preserved at all, is more easily controlled through its own citizens than in any other way.

We have examples of all these methods in the histories of the Spartans and the Romans. The Spartans held Athens and Thebes by creating oligarchies in these cities, yet lost them in the end. The Romans, to retain Capua, Carthage, and Numantia, destroyed them and never lost them. On the other hand, when they thought to hold Greece as the Spartans had held it, leaving it its freedom and allowing it to be governed by its own laws, they failed, and had to destroy many cities of that Province before they could secure it. For, in truth, there is no sure way of holding other than by destroying, and whoever becomes master of a City accustomed to live in freedom and does not destroy it, may reckon on being destroyed by it. For if it should rebel, it can always screen itself under the name of liberty and its ancient laws, which no length of time, nor any benefits conferred will ever cause it to forget; and do what you will, and take what care you may, unless the inhabitants be scattered and dispersed, this name, and the old order of things, will never cease to be remembered, but will at once be turned against you whenever misfortune overtakes you, as when Pisa rose against the Florentines after a hundred years of servitude.

If, however, the newly acquired City or Province has been accustomed to live under a Prince, and his line is extinguished, it will be impossible for the citizens, used, on the one hand, to obey, and deprived, on the other, of their old ruler, to agree to choose a leader from among themselves; and as they know not how to live as freemen, and are therefore slow to take up arms, a stranger may readily gain them over and attach them to his cause. But in Republics there is a stronger vitality, a fiercer hatred, a keener thirst for revenge. The memory of their former freedom will not let them rest; so that the safest course is either to destroy them, or to go and live in them.

Chapter VI.

Of New Princedoms Which a Prince Acquires With His Own Arms and by Merit

Let no man marvel if in what I am about to say concerning Princedoms wholly new, both as regards the Prince and the form of Government, I cite the highest examples. For since men for the most part follow in the footsteps and imitate the actions of others, and yet are unable to adhere exactly to those paths which others have taken, or attain to the virtues of those whom they would resemble, the wise man should always follow the roads that have been trodden by the great, and imitate those who have most excelled, so that if he cannot reach their perfection, he may at least acquire something of its savour. Acting in this like the skillful archer, who seeing that the object he would hit is distant, and knowing the range of his bow, takes aim much above the destined mark; not designing that his arrow should strike so high, but that flying high it may alight at the point intended.

I say, then, that in entirely new Princedoms where the Prince himself is new, the difficulty of maintaining possession varies with the greater or less ability of him who acquires possession. And, because the mere fact of a private person rising to be a Prince presupposes either merit or good fortune, it will be seen that the presence of one or other of these two conditions lessens, to some extent, many difficulties. And yet, he who is less beholden to Fortune has often in the end the better success; and it may be for the advantage of a Prince that, from his having no other territories, he is obliged to reside in person in the State which he has acquired.

Looking first to those who have become Princes by their merit and not by their good fortune, I say that the most excellent among them are Moses, Cyrus, Romulus, Theseus, and the like. And though perhaps I ought not to name Moses, he being merely an instrument for carrying out the Divine commands, he is still to be admired for those qualities which made him worthy to converse with God. But if we consider Cyrus and the others who have acquired or founded kingdoms, they will all be seen to be admirable. And if their actions and the particular institutions of which they were the authors be studied, they will be found not to differ from those of Moses, instructed though he was by so great a teacher. Moreover, on examining their lives and actions, we shall see that they were debtors to Fortune for nothing beyond the opportunity which enabled them to shape things as they pleased, without which the force of their spirit would have been spent in vain; as on the other hand, opportunity would have offered itself in vain, had the capacity for turning it to account been wanting. It was necessary, therefore, that Moses should find the children of Israel in bondage in Egypt, and oppressed by the Egyptians, in order that they might be disposed to follow him, and so escape from their servitude. It was fortunate for Romulus that he found no home in Alba, but was exposed at the time of his birth, to the end that he might become king and founder of the City of Rome. It was necessary that Cyrus should find the Persians discontented with the rule of the Medes, and the Medes enervated and effeminate from a prolonged peace. Nor could Theseus have displayed his great qualities had he not found the Athenians disunited and dispersed. But while it was their opportunities that made these men fortunate, it was their own merit that enabled them to recognize these opportunities and turn them to account, to the glory and prosperity of their country.

They who come to the Princedom, as these did, by virtuous paths, acquire with difficulty, but keep with ease. The difficulties which they have in acquiring arise mainly from the new laws and institutions which they are forced to introduce in founding and securing their government. And let it be noted that there is no more delicate matter to take in hand, nor more dangerous to conduct, nor more doubtful in its success, than to set up as a leader in the introduction of changes. For he who innovates will have for his enemies all those who are well off under the existing order of things, and only lukewarm supporters in those who might be better off under the new. This lukewarm temper arises partly from the fear of adversaries who have the laws on their side, and partly from the incredulity of mankind, who will never admit the merit of anything new, until they have seen it proved by the event. The result, however, is that whenever the enemies of change make an attack, they do so with all the zeal of partisans, while the others defend themselves so feebly as to endanger both themselves and their cause.

But to get a clearer understanding of this part of our subject, we must look whether these innovators can stand alone, or whether they depend for aid upon others; in other words, whether to carry out their ends they must resort to entreaty, or can prevail by force. In the former case they always fare badly and bring nothing to a successful issue; but when they depend upon their own resources and can employ force, they seldom fail. Hence it comes that all armed Prophets have been victorious, and all unarmed Prophets have been destroyed.

For, besides what has been said, it should be borne in mind that the temper of the multitude is fickle, and that while it is easy to persuade them of a thing, it is hard to fix them in that persuasion. Wherefore, matters should be so ordered that when men no longer believe of their own accord, they may be compelled to believe by force. Moses, Cyrus, Theseus, and Romulus could never have made their ordinances be observed for any length of time had they been unarmed, as was the case, in our own days, with the Friar Girolamo Savonarola, whose new institutions came to nothing so soon as the multitude began to waver in their faith; since he had not the means to keep those who had been believers steadfast in their belief, or to make unbelievers believe.

Such persons, therefore, have great difficulty in carrying out their designs; but all their difficulties are on the road, and may be overcome by courage. Having conquered these, and coming to be held in reverence, and having destroyed all who were jealous of their influence, they remain powerful, safe, honoured, and prosperous.

To the great examples cited above, I would add one other, of less note indeed, but assuredly bearing some proportion to them, and which may stand for all others of a like character. I mean the example of Hiero the Syracusan. He from a private station rose to be Prince of Syracuse, and he too was indebted to Fortune only for his opportunity. For the Syracusans being oppressed, chose him to be their Captain, which office he so discharged as deservedly to be made their King. For

44 Chapter VII.

even while a private citizen his merit was so remarkable, that one who writes of him says, he lacked nothing that a King should have save the Kingdom. Doing away with the old army, he organized a new, abandoned existing alliances and assumed new allies, and with an army and allies of his own, was able on that foundation to build what superstructure he pleased; having trouble enough in acquiring, but none in preserving what he had acquired.

Chapter VII.

Of New Princedoms Acquired By the Aid of Others and By Good Fortune

They who from a private station become Princes by mere good fortune, do so with little trouble, but have much trouble to maintain themselves. They meet with no hindrance on their way, being carried as it were on wings to their destination, but all their difficulties overtake them when they alight. Of this class are those on whom States are conferred either in return for money, or through the favour of him who confers them; as it happened to many in the Greek cities of Ionia and the Hellespont to be made Princes by Darius, that they might hold these cities for his security and glory; and as happened in the case of those Emperors who, from privacy, attained the Imperial dignity by corrupting the army. Such Princes are wholly dependent on the favour and fortunes of those who have made them great, than which supports none could be less stable or secure; and they lack both the knowledge and the power that would enable them to maintain their position. They lack the knowledge, because unless they have great parts and force of character, it is not to be expected that having always lived in a private station they should have learned how to command. They lack the power, since they cannot look for support from attached and faithful troops. Moreover, States suddenly acquired, like all else that is produced and that grows up rapidly, can never have such root or hold as that the first storm which strikes them shall not overthrow them; unless, indeed, as I have said already, they who thus suddenly become Princes have a capacity for learning quickly how to defend what Fortune has placed in their lap, and can lay those foundations after they rise which by others are laid before.

Of each of these methods of becoming a Prince, namely, by merit and by good fortune, I shall select an instance from times within my own recollection, and shall take the cases of Francesco Sforza and Cesare Borgia. By suitable measures and singular ability, Francesco Sforza rose from privacy to be Duke of Milan, preserving with little trouble what it cost him infinite efforts to gain. On the other hand, Cesare Borgia, vulgarly spoken of as Duke Valentino, obtained his

Princedom through the favourable fortunes of his father, and with these lost it, although, so far as in him lay, he used every effort and practised every expedient that a prudent and able man should, who desires to strike root in a State given him by the arms and fortune of another. For, as I have already said, he who does not lay his foundations at first, may, if he be of great parts, succeed in laying them afterwards, though with inconvenience to the builder and risk to the building. And if we consider the various measures taken by Duke Valentino, we shall perceive how broad were the foundations he had laid whereon to rest his future power.

These I think it not superfluous to examine, since I know not what lessons I could teach a new Prince, more useful than the example of his actions. And if the measures taken by him did not profit him in the end, it was through no fault of his, but from the extraordinary and extreme malignity of Fortune.

In his efforts to aggrandize the Duke his son, Alexander VI had to face many difficulties, both immediate and remote. In the first place, he saw no way to make him Lord of any State which was not a State of the Church, while, if he sought to take for him a State belonging to the Church, he knew that the Duke of Milan and the Venetians would withhold their consent; Faenza and Rimini being already under the protection of the latter. Further, he saw that the arms of Italy, and those more especially of which he might have availed himself, were in the hands of men who had reason to fear his aggrandizement, that is, of the Orsini, the Colonnesi, and their followers. These therefore he could not trust. It was consequently necessary that the existing order of things should be changed, and the States of Italy thrown into confusion, in order that he might safely make himself master of some part of them; and this became easy for him when he found that the Venetians, moved by other causes, were plotting to bring the French once more into Italy. This design he accordingly did not oppose, but furthered by annulling the first marriage of the French King.

King Louis therefore came into Italy at the instance of the Venetians, and with the consent of Pope Alexander, and no sooner was he in Milan than the Pope got troops from him to aid him in his enterprise against Romagna, which Province, moved by the reputation of the French arms, at once submitted. After thus obtaining possession of Romagna, and after quelling the Colonnesi, Duke Valentino was desirous to follow up and extend his conquests. Two causes, however, held him back, namely, the doubtful fidelity of his own forces, and the waywardness of France. For he feared that the Orsini, of whose arms he had made use, might fail him, and not merely prove a hindrance to further acquisitions, but take from him what he had gained, and that the King might serve him the same turn. How little he could count on the Orsini was made plain when, after the capture of Faenza, he turned his arms against Bologna, and saw how reluctantly they took part in that enterprise. The King's mind he understood, when, after seizing on the Dukedom of Urbino, he was about to attack Tuscany; from which design Louis compelled him to desist. Whereupon the Duke resolved to depend no longer on the arms or fortune of others. His first step, therefore, was to weaken the factions of the Orsini and Colonnesi in Rome. Those of their following who were of good birth, he gained over by making them his own gentlemen, assigning them a liberal provision, and conferring upon them commands and appointments suited to their rank; so that in a few months their old partisan attachments died out, and the hopes of all rested on the Duke alone.

He then awaited an occasion to crush the chiefs of the Orsini, for those of the house of Colonna he had already scattered, and a good opportunity presenting itself, he turned it to the best account. For when the Orsini came at last to see that the greatness of the Duke and the Church involved their ruin, they assembled a council at Magione in the Perugian territory, whence resulted the revolt of Urbino, commotions in Romagna, and an infinity of dangers to the Duke, all of which he overcame with the help of France. His credit thus restored, the Duke trusting no longer either to the French or to any other foreign aid, that he might not have to confront them openly, resorted to stratagem, and was so well able to dissemble his designs, that the Orsini, through the mediation of Signor Paolo (whom he failed not to secure by every friendly attention, furnishing him with clothes, money, and horses), were so won over as to be drawn in their simplicity into his hands at Sinigaglia. When the leaders were thus disposed of, and their followers made his friends, the Duke had laid sufficiently good foundations for his future power, since he held all Romagna together with the Dukedom of Urbino, and had ingratiated himself with the entire population of these States, who now began to see that they were well off.

And since this part of his conduct merits both attention and imitation, I shall not pass it over in silence. After the Duke had taken Romagna, finding that it had been ruled by feeble Lords, who thought more of plundering than correcting their subjects, and gave them more cause for division than for union, so that the country was overrun with robbery, tumult, and every kind of outrage, he judged it necessary, with a view to render it peaceful and obedient to his authority, to provide it with a good government. Accordingly he set over it Messer Remiro d'Orco, a stern and prompt ruler, who being entrusted with the fullest powers, in a very short time, and with much credit to himself, restored it to tranquillity and order. But afterwards apprehending that such unlimited authority might become odious, the Duke decided that it was no longer needed, and established in the center of the Province a civil Tribunal, with an excellent President, in which every town was represented by its advocate. And knowing that past severities had generated ill-feeling against himself, in order to purge the minds of the people and gain their good-will, he sought to show them that any cruelty which had been done had not originated, with him, but in the harsh disposition of his minister. Availing himself of the pretext which this afforded, he one morning caused Remiro to be beheaded, and exposed in the market place of Cesena with a block and bloody axe by his side. The barbarity of which spectacle at once astounded and satisfied the populace.

But, returning to the point whence we diverged, I say that the Duke, finding himself fairly strong and in a measure secured against present dangers, being furnished with arms of his own choosing and having to a great extent got rid of those which, if left near him, might have caused him trouble, had to consider, if he desired to follow up his conquests, how he was to deal with France, since he saw he could expect no further support from King Louis, whose eyes were at last opened to his mistake. He therefore began to look about for new alliances, and to waver in his adherence to the French, then occupied with their expedition into the kingdom of Naples against the Spaniards, at that time laying siege to Gaeta; his object being to secure himself against France; and in this he would soon have succeeded had Alexander lived.

Such was the line he took to meet present exigencies. As regards the future, he had to apprehend that a new Head of the Church might not be his friend, and might even seek to deprive him of what Alexander had given. This he thought to provide against in four ways. First, by exterminating all who were of kin to those Lords whom he had despoiled of their possessions, that they might not become instruments in the hands of a new Pope. Second, by gaining over all the Roman nobles, so as to be able with their help to put a bridle, as the saying is, in the Pope's mouth. Third, by bringing the college of Cardinals, so far as he could, under his control. And fourth, by establishing his authority so firmly before his father's death, as to be able by himself to withstand the shock of a first onset.

Of these measures, at the time when Alexander died, he had already effected three, and had almost carried out the forth. For of the Lords whose possessions he had usurped, he had put to death all whom he could reach, and very few had escaped. He had gained over the Roman nobility, and had the majority in the College of Cardinals on his side.

As to further acquisitions, his design was to make himself master of Tuscany. He was already in possession of Perugia and Piombino, and had assumed the protectorship of Pisa, on which city he was about to spring; taking no heed of France, as indeed he no longer had occasion, since the French had been deprived of the kingdom of Naples by the Spaniards under circumstances which made it necessary for both nations to buy his friendship. Pisa taken, Lucca and Siena would soon have yielded, partly through jealousy of Florence, partly through fear, and the position of the Florentines must then have been desperate.

Had he therefore succeeded in these designs, as he was succeeding in that very year in which Alexander died, he would have won such power and reputation that he might afterwards have stood alone, relying on his own strength and resources, without being beholden to the power and fortune of others. But Alexander died five years from the time he first unsheathed the sword, leaving his son with the State of Romagna alone consolidated, with all the rest unsettled, between two powerful hostile armies, and sick almost to death. And yet such were the fire and courage of the Duke, he knew so well how men must either be conciliated or crushed, and so solid were the foundations he had laid in that brief period, that had these armies not been upon his back, or had he been in sound health, he must have surmounted every difficulty.

How strong his foundations were may be seen from this, that Romagna waited for him for more than a month; and that although half dead, he remained in safety in Rome, where though the Baglioni, the Vitelli, and the Orsini came to attack him, they met with no success. Moreover, since he was able if not to make whom he liked Pope, at least to prevent the election of any whom he disliked, had he been in health at the time when Alexander died, all would have been easy for him. But he told me himself on the day on which Julius II was created, that he had foreseen and provided for everything else that could happen on his father's death, but had never anticipated that when his father died he too should be at death's-door.

Taking all these actions of the Duke together, I can find no fault with him; nay, it seems to me reasonable to put him forward, as I have done, as a pattern for all such as rise to power by good fortune and the help of others. For with his great spirit and high aims he could not act otherwise than he did, and nothing but the shortness of his father's life and his own illness prevented the success of his designs. Whoever, therefore, on entering a new Princedom, judges it necessary to rid himself of enemies, to conciliate friends, to prevail by force or fraud, to make himself feared yet not hated by his subjects, respected and obeyed by his soldiers, to crush those who can or ought to injure him, to introduce changes in the old order of things, to be at once severe and affable, magnanimous and liberal, to do away with a mutinous army and create a new one, to maintain relations with Kings and Princes on such a footing that they must see it for their interest to aid him, and dangerous to offend, can find no brighter example than in the actions of this Prince.

The one thing for which he may be blamed was the creation of Pope Julius II, in respect of whom he chose badly. Because, as I have said already, though he could not secure the election he desired, he could have prevented any other; and he ought never to have consented to the creation of any one of those Cardinals whom he had injured, or who on becoming Pope would have reason to fear him; for fear is as dangerous an enemy as resentment. Those whom he had offended were, among others, San Pietro ad Vincula, Colonna, San Giorgio, and Ascanio; all the rest, excepting d'Amboise and the Spanish Cardinals (the latter from their connexion and obligations, the former from the power he derived through his relations with the French Court), would on assuming the Pontificate have had reason to fear him. The duke, therefore, ought, in the first place, to have laboured for the creation of a Spanish Pope; failing in which, he should have agreed to the election of d'Amboise, but never to that of San Pietro ad Vincula. And he deceives himself who believes that with the great, recent benefits cause old wrongs to be forgotten.

The Duke, therefore, erred in the part he took in this election; and his error was the cause of his ultimate downfall.

Chapter VIII.

Of Those Who By Their Crimes Come to Be Princes

But since from privacy a man may also rise to be a Prince in one or other of two ways, neither of which can be referred wholly either to merit or to fortune, it is fit that I notice them here, though one of them may fall to be discussed more fully in treating of Republics.

The ways I speak of are, first, when the ascent to power is made by paths of wickedness and crime; and second, when a private person becomes ruler of his country by the favour of his fellow-citizens. The former method I shall make clear by two examples, one ancient, the other modern, without entering further into the merits of the matter, for these, I think, should be enough for anyone who is driven to follow them.

Agathocles the Sicilian came, not merely from a private station, but from the very dregs of the people, to be King of Syracuse. Son of a potter, through all the stages of his fortunes he led a foul life. His vices, however, were conjoined with so great vigour both of mind and body, that becoming a soldier, he rose through the various grades of the service to be Praetor of Syracuse. Once established in that post, he resolved to make himself Prince, and to hold by violence and without obligation to others the authority which had been spontaneously entrusted to him. Accordingly, after imparting his design to Hamilcar, who with the Carthaginian armies was at that time waging war in Sicily, he one morning assembled the people and senate of Syracuse as though to consult with them on matters of public moment, and on a preconcerted signal caused his soldiers to put to death all the senators, and the wealthiest of the commons. These being thus got rid of, he assumed and retained possession of the sovereignty without opposition on the part of the people; and although twice defeated by the Carthaginians, and afterwards besieged, he was able not only to defend his city, but leaving a part of his forces for its protection, to invade Africa with the remainder, and so in a short time to raise the siege of Syracuse, reducing the Carthaginians to the utmost extremities, and compelling them to make terms whereby they abandoned Sicily to him and confined themselves to Africa.

Whoever examines this man's actions and achievements will discover little or nothing in them which can be ascribed to Fortune, seeing, as has already been said, that it was not through the favour of any, but by the regular steps of the military service, gained at the cost of a thousand hardships and hazards, he reached the princedom which he afterwards maintained by so many daring and dangerous enterprises. Still, to slaughter fellow-citizens, to betray friends, to be devoid of honour, pity, and religion, cannot be counted as merits, for these are means which may lead to power, but which confer no glory. Wherefore, if in respect of the valour with which he encountered and extricated himself from difficulties, and the constancy of his spirit in supporting and conquering adverse fortune, there seems no reason to judge him inferior to the greatest captains that have ever lived, his unbridled cruelty and inhumanity, together with his countless crimes, forbid us to number him with the greatest men; but, at any rate, we cannot attribute to Fortune or to merit what he accomplished without either.

In our own times, during the papacy of Alexander VI, Oliverotto of Fermo, who some years before had been left an orphan, and had been brought up by his maternal uncle Giovanni Fogliani, was sent while still a lad to serve under Paolo Vitelli, in the expectation that a thorough training under that commander might qualify him for high rank as a soldier. After the death of Paolo, he served under his brother Vitellozzo, and in a very short time, being of a quick wit, hardy and resolute, he became one of the first soldiers of his company. But thinking it beneath him to serve under others, with the countenance of the Vitelleschi and the connivance of certain citizens of Fermo who preferred the slavery to the freedom of their country, he formed the design to seize on that town.

He accordingly wrote to Giovanni Fogliani that after many years of absence from home, he desired to see him and his native city once more, and to look a little into the condition of his patrimony; and as his one endeavour had been to make himself a name, in order that his fellow-citizens might see his time had not been misspent, he proposed to return honourably attended by a hundred horsemen from among his own friends and followers; and he begged Giovanni graciously to arrange for his reception by the citizens of Fermo with corresponding marks of distinction, as this would be creditable not only to himself, but also to the uncle who had brought him up.

Giovanni accordingly, did not fail in any proper attention to his nephew, but caused him to be splendidly received by his fellow-citizens, and lodged him in his house; where Oliverotto having passed some days, and made the necessary arrangements for carrying out his wickedness, gave a formal banquet, to which he invited his uncle and all the first men of Fermo. When the repast and the other entertainments proper to such an occasion had come to an end, Oliverotto artfully turned the conversation to matters of grave interest, by speaking of the greatness of Pope Alexander and Cesare his son, and of their enterprises; and when Giovanni and the others were replying to what he said, he suddenly rose up, observing that these were matters to be discussed in a more private place, and so withdrew to another chamber; whither his uncle and all the other citizens followed him, and where they had no sooner seated themselves, than soldiers rushing out from places of concealment put Giovanni and all the rest to death.

After this butchery, Oliverotto mounted his horse, rode through the streets, and besieged the chief magistrate in the palace, so that all were constrained by fear to yield obedience and accept a government of which he made himself the head. And all who from being disaffected were likely to stand in his way, he put to death, while he strengthened himself with new ordinances, civil and military, to such purpose, that for the space of a year during which he retained the Princedom, he not merely kept a firm hold of the city, but grew formidable to all his neighbours. And it would have been as impossible to unseat him as it was to unseat Agathocles, had he not let himself be overreached by Cesare Borgia on the occasion when, as has already been told, the Orsini and Vitelli were entrapped at Sinigaglia; where he too being taken, one year after the commission of his parricidal crime, was strangled along with Vitellozzo, whom he had assumed for his master in villany as in valour.

It may be asked how Agathocles and some like him, after numberless acts of treachery and cruelty, have been able to live long in their own country in safety, and to defend themselves from foreign enemies, without being plotted against by their fellow-citizens, whereas, many others, by reason of their cruelty, have failed to maintain their position even in peaceful times, not to speak of the perilous times of war. I believe that this results from cruelty being well or ill-employed. Those cruelties we may say are well employed, if it be permitted to speak well of things evil, which are done once for all under the necessity of self-preservation, and are not afterwards persisted in, but so far as possible modified to the advantage of the governed. Ill-employed cruelties, on the other hand, are those which from small beginnings increase rather than diminish with time. They who follow the first of these methods, may, by the grace of God and man, find, as did Agathocles, that their condition is not desperate; but by no possibility can the others maintain themselves.

Hence we may learn the lesson that on seizing a state, the usurper should make haste to inflict what injuries he must, at a stroke, that he may not have to renew them daily, but be enabled by their discontinuance to reassure men's minds, and afterwards win them over by benefits. Whosoever, either through timidity or from following bad counsels, adopts a contrary course, must keep the sword always drawn, and can put no trust in his subjects, who suffering from continued and constantly renewed severities, will never yield him their confidence. Injuries, therefore, should be inflicted all at once, that their ill savour being less lasting may the less offend; whereas, benefits should be conferred little by little, that so they may be more fully relished.

But, before all things, a Prince should so live with his subjects that no vicissitude of good or evil fortune shall oblige him to alter his behaviour; because, if a need to change come through adversity, it is then too late to resort to severity; while any leniency you may use will be thrown away, for it will be seen to be compulsory and gain you no thanks.

Chapter IX.

Of the Civil Princedom

I come now to the second case, namely, of the leading citizen who, not by crimes or violence, but by the favour of his fellow-citizens is made Prince of his country. This may be called a Civil Princedom, and its attainment depends not wholly on merit, nor wholly on good fortune, but rather on what may be termed a *fortunate astuteness*. I say then that the road to this Princedom lies either through the favour of the people or of the nobles. For in every city are to be found these two opposed humours having their origin in this, that the people desire not to be domineered over or oppressed by the nobles, while the nobles desire to oppress and domineer over the people. And from these two contrary appetites there arises in cities one of three results, a Princedom, or Liberty, or Licence. A Princedom is created either by the people or by the nobles, according as one or other of these factions has occasion for it. For when the nobles perceive that they cannot withstand the people, they set to work to magnify the reputation of one of their number, and make him their Prince, to the end that under his shadow they may be enabled to indulge their desires. The people, on the other hand, when they see that they cannot make head against the nobles, invest a single citizen with all their influence and make him Prince, that they may have the shelter of his authority.

He who is made Prince by the favour of the nobles, has greater difficulty to maintain himself than he who comes to the Princedom by aid of the people, since he finds many about him who think themselves as good as he, and whom, on that account, he cannot guide or govern as he would. But he who reaches the Princedom by the popular support, finds himself alone, with none, or but a very few about him who are not ready to obey. Moreover, the demands of the nobles cannot be satisfied with credit to the Prince, nor without injury to others, while those of the people well may, the aim of the people being more honourable than that of the nobles, the latter seeking to oppress, the former not to be oppressed. Add to this, that a Prince can never secure himself against a disaffected people, their number being too great, while he may against a disaffected nobility, since their number is small. The worst that a Prince need fear from a disaffected people is, that they may desert him, whereas when the nobles are his enemies he has to fear not only that they may desert him, but also that they may turn against him; because, as they have greater craft and foresight, they always choose their time to suit their safety, and seek favour with the side they think will win. Again, a Prince must always live with the same people, but need not always live with the same nobles, being able to make and unmake these from day to day, and give and take away their authority at his pleasure.

But to make this part of the matter clearer, I say that as regards the nobles there is this first distinction to be made. They either so govern their conduct as to bind themselves wholly to your fortunes, or they do not. Those who so bind themselves, and who are not grasping, should be loved and honoured. As to those who do not so bind themselves, there is this further distinction. For the most part they are held back by pusillanimity and a natural defect of courage, in which case you should make use of them, and of those among them more especially who are prudent, for they will do you honour in prosperity, and in adversity give you no cause for fear. But where they abstain from attaching themselves to you of set purpose and for ambitious ends, it is a sign that they are thinking more of themselves than of you, and against such men a Prince should be on his guard, and treat them as though they were declared enemies, for in his adversity they will always help to ruin him.

He who becomes a Prince through the favour of the people should always keep on good terms with them; which it is easy for him to do, since all they ask is not to be oppressed. But he who against the will of the people is made a Prince by the favour of the nobles, must, above all things, seek to conciliate the people, which he readily may by taking them under his protection. For since men who are well treated by one whom they expected to treat them ill, feel the more beholden to their benefactor, the people will at once become better disposed to such a Prince when he protects them, than if he owed his Princedom to them.

There are many ways in which a Prince may gain the good-will of the people, but, because these vary with circumstances, no certain rule can be laid down respecting them, and I shall, therefore, say no more about them. But this is the sum of the matter, that it is essential for a Prince to be on a friendly footing with his people, since otherwise, he will have no resource in adversity. Nabis, Prince of Sparta, was attacked by the whole hosts of Greece, and by a Roman army flushed with victory, and defended his country and crown against them; and when danger approached, there were but few of his subjects against whom he needed to guard himself, whereas had the people been hostile, this would not have been enough.

And what I affirm let no one controvert by citing the old saw that *'he who builds on the people builds on mire,'* for that may be true of a private citizen who presumes on his favour with the people, and counts on being rescued by them when overpowered by his enemies or by the magistrates. In such cases a man may often find himself deceived, as happened to the Gracchi in Rome, and in Florence to Messer Giorgio Scali. But when he who builds on the people is a Prince capable of command, of a spirit not to be cast down by ill-fortune, who, while he animates the whole community by his courage and bearing, neglects no prudent precaution, he will not find himself betrayed by the people, but will be seen to have laid his foundations well.

The most critical juncture for Princedoms of this kind, is at the moment when they are about to pass from the popular to the absolute form of government: and as these Princes exercise their authority either directly or through the agency of the magistrates, in the latter case their position is weaker and more hazardous, since they are wholly in the power of those citizens to whom the magistracies are entrusted, who can, and especially in difficult times, with the greatest ease deprive them of their authority, either by opposing, or by not obeying them. And in times of peril it is too late for a Prince to assume to himself an absolute authority, for the citizens and subjects who are accustomed to take their orders from the magistrates, will not when dangers threaten take them from the Prince, so that at such seasons there will always be very few in whom he can trust. Such Princes, therefore, must not build on what they see in tranquil times when the citizens feel the need of the State. For then everyone is ready to run, to promise, and, danger of death being remote, even to die for the State. But in troubled times, when the State has need of its citizens, few of them are to be found. And the risk of the experiment is the greater in that it can only be made once. Wherefore, a wise Prince should devise means whereby his subjects may at all times, whether favourable or adverse, feel the need of the State and of him, and then they will always be faithful to him.

Chapter X.

How the Strength of All Princedoms Should Be Measured

In examining the character of these Princedoms, another circumstance has to be considered, namely, whether the Prince is strong enough, if occasion demands, to stand alone, or whether he needs continual help from others. To make the matter clearer, I pronounce those to be able to stand alone who, with the men and money at their disposal, can get together an army fit to take the field against any assailant; and, conversely, I judge those to be in constant need of help who cannot take the field against their enemies, but are obliged to retire behind their walls, and to defend themselves there. Of the former I have already spoken, and shall speak again as occasion may require. As to the latter there is nothing to be said, except to exhort such Princes to strengthen and fortify the towns in which they dwell, and take no heed of the country outside. For whoever has thoroughly fortified his town, and put himself on such a footing with his subjects as I have already indicated and shall hereafter speak of, will always be attacked with much circumspection; for men are always averse to enterprises that are attended with difficulty, and it is impossible not to foresee difficulties in attacking a Prince whose town is strongly fortified and who is not hated by his subjects.

The towns of Germany enjoy great freedom. Having little territory, they render obedience to the Emperor only when so disposed, fearing neither him nor any other neighbouring power. For they are so fortified that it is plain to everyone that it would be a tedious and difficult task to reduce them, since all of them are protected by moats and suitable ramparts, are well supplied with artillery, and keep their public magazines constantly stored with victual, drink and fuel, enough to last them for a year. Besides which, in order to support the poorer class of citizens without public loss, they lay in a common stock of materials for these to work on for a year, in the handicrafts which are the life and sinews of such cities, and by which the common people live. Moreover, they esteem military exercises and have many regulations for their maintenance.

A Prince, therefore, who has a strong city, and who does not make himself hated, cannot be attacked, or should he be so, his assailant will come badly off; since human affairs are so variable that it is almost impossible for anyone to keep an army posted in leaguer for a whole year without interruption of some sort. Should it be objected that if the citizens have possessions outside the town, and see them burned, they will lose patience, and that self-interest, together with the hardships of a protracted siege, will cause them to forget their loyalty; I answer that a capable and courageous Prince will always overcome these difficulties, now, by holding out hopes to his subjects that the evil will not be of long continuance; now, by exciting their fears of the enemy's cruelty; and, again, by dexterously silencing those who seem to him too forward in their complaints. Moreover, it is to be expected that the enemy will burn and lay waste the country immediately on their arrival, at a time when men's minds are still heated and resolute for defence. And for this very reason the Prince ought the less to fear, because after a few days, when the first ardour has abated, the injury is already done and suffered, and cannot be undone; and the people will now, all the more readily, make common cause with their Prince from his seeming to be under obligations to them, their houses having been burned and their lands wasted in his defence. For it is the nature of men to incur obligation as much by the benefits they render as by those they receive.

Wherefore, if the whole matter be well considered, it ought not to be difficult for a prudent Prince, both at the outset and afterwards, to maintain the spirits of his subjects during a siege; provided always that victuals and other means of defence do not run short.

Chapter XI.

Of Ecclesiastical Princedoms

It now only remains for me to treat of Ecclesiastical Princedoms, all the difficulties in respect of which precede their acquisition. For they are acquired by merit or good fortune, but are maintained without either; being upheld by the venerable ordinances of Religion, which are all of such a nature and efficacy that they secure the authority of their Princes in whatever way they may act or live. These Princes alone have territories which they do not defend, and subjects whom they do not govern; yet their territories are not taken from them through not being defended, nor are their subjects concerned at not being governed, or led to think of throwing off their allegiance; nor is it in their power to do so. Accordingly these Princedoms alone are secure and happy. But inasmuch as they are sustained by agencies of a higher nature than the mind of man can reach, I forbear to speak of them: for since they are set up and supported by God himself, he would be a rash and presumptuous man who should venture to discuss them.

Nevertheless, should any one ask me how it comes about that the temporal power of the Church, which before the time of Alexander was looked on with contempt by all the Potentates of Italy, and not only by those so styling themselves, but by every Baron and Lordling however insignificant, has now reached such a pitch of greatness that the King of France trembles before it, and that it has been able to drive him out of

Italy and to crush the Venetians; though the causes be known, it seems to me not superfluous to call them in some measure to recollection.

Before Charles of France passed into Italy, that country was under the control of the Pope, the Venetians, the King of Naples, the Duke of Milan, and the Florentines. Two chief objects had to be kept in view by all these powers: first, that no armed foreigner should be allowed to invade Italy; second, that no one of their own number should be suffered to extend his territory. Those whom it was especially needed to guard against, were the Pope and the Venetians. To hold back the Venetians it was necessary that all the other States should combine, as was done for the defence of Ferrara; while to restrain the Pope, use was made of the Roman Barons, who being divided into two factions, the Orsini and Colonnesi, had constant cause for feud with one another, and standing with arms in their hands under the very eyes of the Pontiff, kept the Popedom feeble and insecure.

And although there arose from time to time a courageous Pope like Sixtus, neither his prudence nor his good fortune could free him from these embarrassments. The cause whereof was the shortness of the lives of the Popes. For in the ten years, which was the average duration of a Pope's life, he could barely succeed in humbling one of these factions; so that if, for instance, one Pope had almost exterminated the Colonnesi, he was followed by another, who being the enemy of the Orsini had no time to rid himself of them, but so far from completing the destruction of the Colonnesi, restored them to life. This led to the temporal authority of the Popes being little esteemed in Italy.

Then came Alexander VI, who more than any of his predecessors showed what a Pope could effect with money and arms, achieving by the instrumentality of Duke Valentino, and by taking advantage of the coming of the French into Italy, all those successes which I have already noticed in speaking of the actions of the Duke. And although his object was to aggrandize, not the Church but the Duke, what he did turned to the advantage of the Church, which after his death, and after the Duke had been put out of the way, became the heir of his labours.

After him came Pope Julius, who found the Church strengthened by the possession of the whole of Romagna, and the Roman Barons exhausted and their factions shattered under the blows of Pope Alexander. He found also a way opened for the accumulation of wealth, which before the time of Alexander no one had followed. These advantages Julius not only used but added to. He undertook the conquest of Bologna, the overthrow of the Venetians, and the expulsion of the French from Italy; in all which enterprises he succeeded, and with the greater glory to himself in that whatever he did, was done to strengthen the Church and not to aggrandize any private person. He succeeded, moreover, in keeping the factions of the Orsini and Colonnesi within the same limits as he found them; and, though some

seeds of insubordination may still have been left among them, two
causes operated to hold them in check; first, the great power of the
Church, which overawed them, and second, their being without
Cardinals, who had been the cause of all their disorders. For these
factions while they have Cardinals among them can never be at rest,
since it is they who foment dissension both in Rome and out of it, in
which the Barons are forced to take part, the ambition of the Prelates
thus giving rise to tumult and discord among the Barons.

His Holiness, Pope Leo, has consequently found the Papacy most
powerful; and from him we may hope, that as his predecessors made it
great with arms, he will render it still greater and more venerable by his
benignity and other countless virtues.

Chapter XII.

How Many Different Kinds of Soldiers There Are, and of Mercenaries

Having spoken particularly of all the various kinds of Princedom
whereof at the outset I proposed to treat, considered in some measure
what are the causes of their strength and weakness, and pointed out the
methods by which men commonly seek to acquire them, it now remains
that I should discourse generally concerning the means for attack and
defence of which each of these different kinds of Princedom may make
use.

I have already said that a Prince must lay solid foundations, since
otherwise he will inevitably be destroyed. Now the main foundations of
all States, whether new, old, or mixed, are good laws and good arms.
But since you cannot have the former without the latter, and where you
have the latter, are likely to have the former, I shall here omit all
discussion on the subject of laws, and speak only of arms.

I say then that the arms wherewith a Prince defends his State are
either his own subjects, or they are mercenaries, or they are auxiliaries,
or they are partly one and partly another. Mercenaries and auxiliaries
are at once useless and dangerous, and he who holds his State by means
of mercenary troops can never be solidly or securely seated. For such
troops are disunited, ambitious, insubordinate, treacherous, insolent
among friends, cowardly before foes, and without fear of God or faith
with man. Whenever they are attacked defeat follows; so that in peace
you are plundered by them, in war by your enemies. And this because
they have no tie or motive to keep them in the field beyond their paltry
pay, in return for which it would be too much to expect them to give
their lives. They are ready enough, therefore, to be your soldiers while
you are at peace, but when war is declared they make off and disappear.
I ought to have little difficulty in getting this believed, for the present
ruin of Italy is due to no other cause than her having for many years

trusted to mercenaries, who though heretofore they may have helped the fortunes of some one man, and made a show of strength when matched with one another, have always revealed themselves in their true colours so soon as foreign enemies appeared. Hence it was that Charles of France was suffered to conquer Italy *with chalk*; and he who said our sins were the cause, said truly, though it was not the sins he meant, but those which I have noticed. And as these were the sins of Princes, they it is who have paid the penalty.

But I desire to demonstrate still more clearly the untoward character of these forces. Captains of mercenaries are either able men or they are not. If they are, you cannot trust them, since they will always seek their own aggrandizement, either by overthrowing you who are their master, or by the overthrow of others contrary to your desire. On the other hand, if your captain be not an able man the chances are you will be ruined. And if it be said that whoever has arms in his hands will act in the same way whether he be a mercenary or no, I answer that when arms have to be employed by a Prince or a Republic, the Prince ought to go in person to take command as captain, the Republic should send one of her citizens, and if he prove incapable should change him, but if he prove capable should by the force of the laws confine him within proper bounds. And we see from experience that both Princes and Republics when they depend on their own arms have the greatest success, whereas from employing mercenaries nothing but loss results. Moreover, a Republic trusting to her own forces, is with greater difficulty than one which relies on foreign arms brought to yield obedience to a single citizen. Rome and Sparta remained for ages armed and free. The Swiss are at once the best armed and the freest people in the world.

Of mercenary arms in ancient times we have an example in the Carthaginians, who at the close of their first war with Rome, were well-nigh ruined by their hired troops, although these were commanded by Carthaginian citizens. So too, when, on the death of Epaminondas, the Thebans made Philip of Macedon captain of their army, after gaining a victory for them, he deprived them of their liberty. The Milanese, in like manner, when Duke Filippo died, took Francesco Sforza into their pay to conduct the war against the Venetians. But he, after defeating the enemy at Caravaggio, combined with them to overthrow the Milanese, his masters. His father too while in the pay of Giovanna, Queen of Naples, suddenly left her without troops, obliging her, in order to save her kingdom, to throw herself into the arms of the King of Aragon.

And if it be said that in times past the Venetians and the Florentines have extended their dominions by means of these arms, and that their captains have served them faithfully, without seeking to make themselves their masters, I answer that in this respect the Florentines have been fortunate, because among those valiant captains who might have given them cause for fear, some have not been victorious, some have had rivals, and some have turned their ambition in other directions.

Among those not victorious, was Giovanni Acuto, whose fidelity, since he was unsuccessful, was not put to the proof: but any one may see, that had he been victorious the Florentines must have been entirely in his hands. The Sforzas, again, had constant rivals in the Bracceschi, so that the one following was a check upon the other; moreover, the ambition of Francesco was directed against Milan, while that of Braccio was directed against the Church and the kingdom of Naples. Let us turn, however, to what took place lately. The Florentines chose for their captain Paolo Vitelli, a most prudent commander, who had raised himself from privacy to the highest renown in arms. Had he been successful in reducing Pisa, none can deny that the Florentines would have been completely in his power, for they would have been ruined had he gone over to their enemies, while if they retained him they must have submitted to his will.

Again, as to the Venetians, if we consider the growth of their power, it will be seen that they conducted their affairs with glory and safety so long as their subjects of all ranks, gentle and simple alike, valiantly bore arms in their wars; as they did before they directed their enterprises landwards. But when they took to making war by land, they forsook those methods in which they excelled and were content to follow the customs of Italy.

At first, indeed, in extending their possessions on the mainland, having as yet but little territory and being held in high repute, they had not much to fear from their captains; but when their territories increased, which they did under Carmagnola, they were taught their mistake. For as they had found him a most valiant and skillful leader when, under his command, they defeated the Duke of Milan, and, on the other hand, saw him slack in carrying on the war, they made up their minds that no further victories were to be had under him; and because, through fear of losing what they had gained, they could not discharge him, to secure themselves against him they were forced to put him to death. After him they have had for captains, Bartolommeo of Bergamo, Roberto of San Severino, the Count of Pitigliano, and the like, under whom their danger has not been from victories, but from defeats; as, for instance, at Vaila, where they lost in a single day what it had taken the efforts of eight hundred years to acquire. For the gains resulting from mercenary arms are slow, and late, and inconsiderable, but the losses sudden and astounding.

And since these examples have led me back to Italy, which for many years past has been defended by mercenary arms, I desire to go somewhat deeper into the matter, in order that the causes which led to the adoption of these arms being seen, they may the more readily be corrected. You are to understand, then, that when in these later times the Imperial control began to be rejected by Italy, and the temporal power of the Pope to be more thought of, Italy suddenly split up into a number of separate States. For many of the larger cities took up arms against their nobles, who, with the favour of the Emperor, had before kept them in subjection, and were supported by the Church with a view to add to her temporal authority: while in many others of these cities, private citizens became rulers. Hence Italy, having passed almost entirely into the hands of the Church and of certain Republics, the former made up of priests, the latter of citizens unfamiliar with arms, began to take foreigners into her pay.

The first who gave reputation to this service was Alberigo of Conio in Romagna, from whose school of warlike training descended, among others, Braccio and Sforza, who in their time were the arbiters of Italy; after whom came all those others who down to the present hour have held similar commands, and to whose merits we owe it that our country has been overrun by Charles, plundered by Louis, wasted by Ferdinand, and insulted by the Swiss.

The first object of these mercenaries was to bring foot soldiers into disrepute, in order to enhance the merit of their own followers; and this they did, because lacking territory of their own and depending on their profession for their support, a few foot soldiers gave them no importance, while for a large number they were unable to provide. For these reasons they had recourse to horsemen, a less retinue of whom was thought to confer distinction, and could be more easily maintained. And the matter went to such a length, that in an army of twenty thousand men, not two thousand foot soldiers were to be found. Moreover, they spared no endeavour to relieve themselves and their men from fatigue and danger, not killing one another in battle, but making prisoners who were afterwards released without ransom. They would attack no town by night; those in towns would make no sortie by night against a besieging army. Their camps were without rampart or trench. They had no winter campaigns. All which arrangements were sanctioned by their military rules, contrived by them, as I have said already, to escape fatigue and danger; but the result of which has been to bring Italy into servitude and contempt.

Chapter XIII.

Of Auxiliary, Mixed, and National Arms

The second sort of unprofitable arms are auxiliaries, by whom I mean, troops brought to help and protect you by a potentate whom you summon to your aid; as when in recent times, Pope Julius II observing the pitiful behaviour of his mercenaries at the enterprise of Ferrara, betook himself to auxiliaries, and arranged with Ferdinand of Spain to be supplied with horse and foot soldiers.

Auxiliaries may be excellent and useful soldiers for themselves, but are always hurtful to him who calls them in; for if they are defeated, he is undone, if victorious, he becomes their prisoner. Ancient histories abound with instances of this, but I shall not pass from the example of Pope Julius, which is still fresh in men's minds. It was the height of rashness for him, in his eagerness to gain Ferrara, to throw himself without reserve into the arms of a stranger. Nevertheless, his good fortune came to his rescue, and he had not to reap the fruits of his ill-considered conduct. For after his auxiliaries were defeated at Ravenna, the Swiss suddenly descended and, to their own surprise and that of everyone else, swept the victors out of the country, so that, he neither remained a prisoner with his enemies, they being put to flight, nor with his auxiliaries, because victory was won by other arms than theirs. The Florentines, being wholly without soldiers of their own, brought ten thousand French men-at-arms to the siege of Pisa, thereby incurring greater peril than at any previous time of trouble. To protect himself from his neighbours, the Emperor of Constantinople summoned ten thousand Turkish soldiers into Greece, who, when the war was over, refused to leave, and this was the beginning of the servitude of Greece to the Infidel.

Let him, therefore, who would deprive himself of every chance of success, have recourse to auxiliaries, these being far more dangerous than mercenary arms, bringing ruin with them ready made. For they are united, and wholly under the control of their own officers; whereas, before mercenaries, even after gaining a victory, can do you hurt, longer time and better opportunities are needed; because, as they are made up of separate companies, raised and paid by you, he whom you place in command cannot at once acquire such authority over them as will be injurious to you. In short, with mercenaries your greatest danger is from their inertness and cowardice, with auxiliaries from their valour. Wise Princes, therefore, have always eschewed these arms, and trusted rather to their own, and have preferred defeat with the latter to victory with the former, counting that as no true victory which is gained by foreign aid.

I shall never hesitate to cite the example of Cesare Borgia and his actions. He entered Romagna with a force of auxiliaries, all of them French men-at-arms, with whom he took Imola and Forli. But it appearing to him afterwards that these troops were not to be trusted, he had recourse to mercenaries from whom he thought there would be less danger, and took the Orsini and Vitelli into his pay. But finding these likewise while under his command to be fickle, false, and treacherous, he got rid of them, and fell back on troops of his own raising. And we may readily discern the difference between these various kinds of arms, by observing the different degrees of reputation in which the Duke stood while he depended upon the French alone, when he took the Orsini and Vitelli into his pay, and when he fell back on his own troops and his own resources; for we find his reputation always increasing, and that he was never so well thought of as when everyone perceived him to be sole master of his own forces.

I am unwilling to leave these examples, drawn from what has taken place in Italy and in recent times; and yet I must not omit to notice the case of Hiero of Syracuse, who is one of those whom I have already named. He, as I have before related, being made captain of their armies by the Syracusans, saw at once that a force of mercenary soldiers, supplied by men resembling our Italian *condottieri*, was not serviceable; and as he would not retain and could not disband them, he caused them all to be cut to pieces, and afterwards made war with native soldiers only, without other aid.

And here I would call to mind a passage in the Old Testament as bearing on this point. When David offered himself to Saul to go forth and fight Goliath the Philistine champion, Saul to encourage him armed him with his own armour, which David, so soon as he had put it on, rejected, saying that with these untried arms he could not prevail, and that he chose rather to meet his enemy with only his sling and his sword. In a word, the armour of others is too wide, or too strait for us; it falls off us, or it weighs us down.

Charles VII, the father of Louis XI, who by his good fortune and valour freed France from the English, saw this necessity of strengthening himself with a national army, and drew up ordinances regulating the service both of men-at-arms and of foot soldiers throughout his kingdom. But afterwards his son, King Louis, did away with the national infantry, and began to hire Swiss mercenaries. Which blunder having been followed by subsequent Princes, has been the cause, as the result shows, of the dangers into which the kingdom of France has fallen; for, by enhancing the reputation of the Swiss, the whole of the national troops of France have been deteriorated. For from their infantry being done away with, their men-at-arms are made wholly dependent on foreign assistance, and being accustomed to co-operate with the Swiss, have grown to think they can do nothing without them. Hence the French are no match for the Swiss, and without them cannot succeed against others.

The armies of France, then, are mixed, being partly national and partly mercenary. Armies thus composed are far superior to mere mercenaries or mere auxiliaries, but far inferior to forces purely national. And this example is in itself conclusive, for the realm of France would be invincible if the military ordinances of Charles VII had been retained and extended. But from want of foresight men make changes which relishing well at first do not betray their hidden venom, as I have already observed respecting hectic fever. Nevertheless, the ruler is not truly wise who cannot discern evils before they develop themselves, and this is a faculty given to few.

If we look for the causes which first led to the overthrow of the Roman Empire, they will be found to have had their source in the employment of Gothic mercenaries, for from that hour the strength of the Romans began to wane and all the virtue which went from them passed to the Goths. And, to be brief, I say that without national arms no Princedom is safe, but on the contrary is wholly dependent on Fortune, being without the strength that could defend it in adversity. And it has always been the deliberate opinion of the wise, that nothing is so infirm and fleeting as a reputation for power not founded upon a national army, by which I mean one composed of subjects, citizens, and dependents, all others being mercenary or auxiliary.

The methods to be followed for organizing a national army may readily be ascertained, if the rules above laid down by me, and by which I abide, be well considered, and attention be given to the manner in which Philip, father of Alexander the Great, and many other Princes and Republics have armed and disposed their forces.

Chapter XIV.

Of the Duty of a Prince In Respect of Military Affairs

A Prince, therefore, should have no care or thought but for war, and for the regulations and training it requires, and should apply himself exclusively to this as his peculiar province; for war is the sole art looked for in one who rules, and is of such efficacy that it not merely maintains those who are born Princes, but often enables men to rise to that eminence from a private station; while, on the other hand, we often see that when Princes devote themselves rather to pleasure than to arms, they lose their dominions. And as neglect of this art is the prime cause of such calamities, so to be a proficient in it is the surest way to acquire power. Francesco Sforza, from his renown in arms, rose from privacy to be Duke of Milan, while his descendants, seeking to avoid the hardships and fatigues of military life, from being Princes fell back into privacy. For among other causes of misfortune which your not being armed brings upon you, it makes you despised, and this is one of those reproaches against which, as shall presently be explained, a Prince ought most carefully to guard.

Between an armed and an unarmed man no proportion holds, and it is contrary to reason to expect that the armed man should voluntarily submit to him who is unarmed, or that the unarmed man should stand secure among armed retainers. For with contempt on one side, and distrust on the other, it is impossible that men should work well together. Wherefore, as has already been said, a Prince who is ignorant of military affairs, besides other disadvantages, can neither be respected by his soldiers, nor can he trust them. A Prince, therefore, ought never to allow his attention to be diverted from warlike pursuits, and should occupy himself with them even more in peace than in war. This he can do in two ways, by practice or by study.

As to the practice, he ought, besides keeping his soldiers well trained and disciplined, to be constantly engaged in the chase, that he may inure his body to hardships and fatigue, and gain at the same time a knowledge of places, by observing how the mountains slope, the valleys open, and the plains spread; acquainting himself with the characters of rivers and marshes, and giving the greatest attention to this subject. Such knowledge is useful to him in two ways; for first, he learns thereby to know his own country, and to understand better how it may be defended; and next, from his familiar acquaintance with its localities, he readily comprehends the character of other districts when obliged to observe them for the first time. For the hills, valleys, plains, rivers, and marshes of Tuscany, for example, have a certain resemblance to those elsewhere; so that from a knowledge of the natural features of that province, similar knowledge in respect of other provinces may readily be gained. The Prince who is wanting in this kind of knowledge, is wanting in the first qualification of a good captain for by it he is taught how to surprise an enemy, how to choose an encampment, how to lead his army on a march, how to array it for battle, and how to post it to the best advantage for a siege.

Among the commendations which Philopoemon, Prince of the Achaians, has received from historians is this—that in times of peace he was always thinking of methods of warfare, so that when walking in the country with his friends he would often stop and talk with them on the subject. 'If the enemy,' he would say, 'were posted on that hill, and we found ourselves here with our army, which of us would have the better position? How could we most safely and in the best order advance to meet them? If we had to retreat, what direction should we take? If they retired, how should we pursue?' In this way he put to his friends, as he went along, all the contingencies that can befall an army. He listened to their opinions, stated his own, and supported them with reasons; and from his being constantly occupied with such meditations, it resulted, that when in actual command no complication could ever present itself with which he was not prepared to deal.

As to the mental training of which we have spoken, a Prince should read histories, and in these should note the actions of great men, observe how they conducted themselves in their wars, and examine the causes of their victories and defeats, so as to avoid the latter and imitate them in the former. And above all, he should, as many great men of past ages have done, assume for his models those persons who before his time have been renowned and celebrated, whose deeds and achievements he should constantly keep in mind, as it is related that Alexander the Great sought to resemble Achilles, Cæsar Alexander, and Scipio Cyrus. And anyone who reads the life of this last-named hero, written by Xenophon, recognizes afterwards in the life of Scipio, how much this imitation was the source of his glory, and how nearly in his chastity, affability, kindliness, and generosity, he conformed to the character of Cyrus as Xenophon describes it.

A wise Prince, therefore, should pursue such methods as these, never resting idle in times of peace, but strenuously seeking to turn them to account, so that he may derive strength from them in the hour of danger, and find himself ready should Fortune turn against him, to resist her blows.

Chapter XV.

Of the Qualities In Respect of Which Men, and Most of all Princes, Are Praised or Blamed

It now remains for us to consider what ought to be the conduct and bearing of a Prince in relation to his subjects and friends. And since I know that many have written on this subject, I fear it may be thought presumptuous in me to write of it also; the more so, because in my treatment of it, I depart from the views that others have taken.

But since it is my object to write what shall be useful to whosoever understands it, it seems to me better to follow the real truth of things than an imaginary view of them. For many Republics and Princedoms have been imagined that were never seen or known to exist in reality. And the manner in which we live, and that in which we ought to live, are things so wide asunder, that he who quits the one to betake himself to the other is more likely to destroy than to save himself; since anyone who would act up to a perfect standard of goodness in everything, must be ruined among so many who are not good. It is essential, therefore, for a Prince who desires to maintain his position, to have learned how to be other than good, and to use or not to use his goodness as necessity requires.

Laying aside, therefore, all fanciful notions concerning a Prince, and considering those only that are true, I say that all men when they are spoken of, and Princes more than others from their being set so high, are characterized by some one of those qualities which attach either praise or blame. Thus one is accounted liberal, another miserly (which word I use, rather than *avaricious*, to denote the man who is too sparing of what is his own, *avarice* being the disposition to take wrongfully what is another's); one is generous, another greedy; one cruel, another tender-hearted; one is faithless, another true to his word; one effeminate and cowardly, another high-spirited and courageous; one is courteous, another haughty; one impure, another chaste; one simple, another crafty; one firm, another facile; one grave, another frivolous; one devout, another unbelieving; and the like. Every one, I know, will admit that it would be most laudable for a Prince to be endowed with all of the above qualities that are reckoned good; but since it is impossible for him to possess or constantly practise them all, the conditions of human nature not allowing it, he must be discreet enough to know how to avoid the infamy of those vices that would deprive him of his government, and, if possible, be on his guard also against those which might not deprive him of it; though if he cannot wholly restrain himself, he may with less scruple indulge in the latter. He need never hesitate, however, to incur the reproach of those vices without which his authority can hardly be preserved; for if he well consider the whole matter, he will find that there may be a line of conduct having the appearance of virtue, to follow which would be his ruin, and that there may be another course having the appearance of vice, by following which his safety and well-being are secured.

Chapter XVI.

Of Liberality and Miserliness

Beginning, then, with the first of the qualities above noticed, I say that it may be a good thing to be reputed liberal, but, nevertheless, that liberality without the reputation of it is hurtful; because, though it be worthily and rightly used, still if it be not known, you escape not the reproach of its opposite vice. Hence, to have credit for liberality with the world at large, you must neglect no circumstance of sumptuous display; the result being, that a Prince of a liberal disposition will consume his whole substance in things of this sort, and, after all, be obliged, if he would maintain his reputation for liberality, to burden his subjects with extraordinary taxes, and to resort to confiscations and all the other shifts whereby money is raised. But in this way he becomes hateful to his subjects, and growing impoverished is held in little esteem by any. So that in the end, having by his liberality offended many and obliged few, he is worse off than when he began, and is exposed to all his original dangers. Recognizing this, and endeavouring to retrace his steps, he at once incurs the infamy of miserliness.

A Prince, therefore, since he cannot without injury to himself practise the virtue of liberality so that it may be known, will not, if he be wise, greatly concern himself though he be called miserly. Because in time he will come to be regarded as more and more liberal, when it is seen that through his parsimony his revenues are sufficient; that he is able to defend himself against any who make war on him; that he can engage in enterprises against others without burdening his subjects; and thus exercise liberality towards all from whom he does not take, whose number is infinite, while he is miserly in respect of those only to whom he does not give, whose number is few.

In our own days we have seen no Princes accomplish great results save those who have been accounted miserly. All others have been ruined. Pope Julius II, after availing himself of his reputation for liberality to arrive at the Papacy, made no effort to preserve that reputation when making war on the King of France, but carried on all his numerous campaigns without levying from his subjects a single extraordinary tax, providing for the increased expenditure out of his long-continued savings. Had the present King of Spain been accounted liberal, he never could have engaged or succeeded in so many enterprises.

A Prince, therefore, if he is enabled thereby to forbear from plundering his subjects, to defend himself, to escape poverty and contempt, and the necessity of becoming rapacious, ought to care little though he incur the reproach of miserliness, for this is one of those vices which enable him to reign.

And should any object that Cæsar by his liberality rose to power, and that many others have been advanced to the highest dignities from their having been liberal and so reputed, I reply, 'Either you are already a Prince or you seek to become one; in the former case liberality is hurtful, in the latter it is very necessary that you be thought liberal; Cæsar was one of those who sought the sovereignty of Rome; but if after obtaining it he had lived on without retrenching his expenditure, he must have ruined the Empire.' And if it be further urged that many Princes reputed to have been most liberal have achieved great things with their armies, I answer that a Prince spends either what belongs to himself and his subjects, or what belongs to others; and that in the former case he ought to be sparing, but in the latter ought not to refrain from any kind of liberality. Because for a Prince who leads his armies in person and maintains them by plunder, pillage, and forced contributions, dealing as he does with the property of others this liberality is necessary, since otherwise he would not be followed by his soldiers. Of what does not belong to you or to your subjects you should, therefore, be a lavish giver, as were Cyrus, Cæsar, and Alexander; for to be liberal with the property of others does not take from your reputation, but adds to it. What injures you is to give away what is your own. And there is no quality so self-destructive as liberality; for while you practise it you lose the means whereby it can be practised, and become poor and despised, or else, to avoid poverty, you become rapacious and hated. For liberality leads to one or other of these two results, against which, beyond all others, a Prince should guard.

Wherefore it is wiser to put up with the name of being miserly, which breeds ignominy, but without hate, than to be obliged, from the desire to be reckoned liberal, to incur the reproach of rapacity, which breeds hate as well as ignominy.

Chapter XVII.

Of Cruelty and Clemency, and Whether It Is Better To Be Loved or Feared

Passing to the other qualities above referred to, I say that every Prince should desire to be accounted merciful and not cruel. Nevertheless, he should be on his guard against the abuse of this quality of mercy. Cesare Borgia was reputed cruel, yet his cruelty restored Romagna, united it, and brought it to order and obedience; so that if we look at things in their true light, it will be seen that he was in reality far more merciful than the people of Florence, who, to avoid the imputation of cruelty, suffered Pistoia to be torn to pieces by factions.

A Prince should therefore disregard the reproach of being thought cruel where it enables him to keep his subjects united and obedient. For he who quells disorder by a very few signal examples will in the end be more merciful than he who from too great leniency permits things to take their course and so to result in rapine and bloodshed; for these hurt the whole State, whereas the severities of the Prince injure individuals only.

And for a new Prince, of all others, it is impossible to escape a name for cruelty, since new States are full of dangers. Wherefore Virgil, by the mouth of Dido, excuses the harshness of her reign on the plea that it was new, saying:—

'A fate unkind, and newness in my reign
Compel me thus to guard a wide domain.'

Nevertheless, the new Prince should not be too ready of belief, nor too easily set in motion; nor should he himself be the first to raise alarms; but should so temper prudence with kindliness that too great confidence in others shall not throw him off his guard, nor groundless distrust render him insupportable.

And here comes in the question whether it is better to be loved rather than feared, or feared rather than loved. It might perhaps be answered that we should wish to be both; but since love and fear can hardly exist together, if we must choose between them, it is far safer to be feared than loved. For of men it may generally be affirmed, that they are thankless, fickle, false studious to avoid danger, greedy of gain, devoted to you while you are able to confer benefits upon them, and ready, as I said before, while danger is distant, to shed their blood, and sacrifice their property, their lives, and their children for you; but in the hour of need they turn against you. The Prince, therefore, who without otherwise securing himself builds wholly on their professions is undone. For the friendships which we buy with a price, and do not gain by greatness and nobility of character, though they be fairly earned are not made good, but fail us when we have occasion to use them.

Moreover, men are less careful how they offend him who makes himself loved than him who makes himself feared. For love is held by the tie of obligation, which, because men are a sorry breed, is broken on every whisper of private interest; but fear is bound by the apprehension of punishment which never relaxes its grasp.

Nevertheless a Prince should inspire fear in such a fashion that if he does not win love he may escape hate. For a man may very well be feared and yet not hated, and this will be the case so long as he does not meddle with the property or with the women of his citizens and subjects. And if constrained to put any to death, he should do so only when there is manifest cause or reasonable justification. But, above all, he must abstain from the property of others. For men will sooner forget the death of their father than the loss of their patrimony. Moreover, pretexts for confiscation are never to seek, and he who has once begun to live by rapine always finds reasons for taking what is not his; whereas reasons for shedding blood are fewer, and sooner exhausted.

But when a Prince is with his army, and has many soldiers under his command, he must needs disregard the reproach of cruelty, for without such a reputation in its Captain, no army can be held together or kept under any kind of control. Among other things remarkable in Hannibal this has been noted, that having a very great army, made up of men of many different nations and brought to fight in a foreign country, no dissension ever arose among the soldiers themselves, nor any mutiny against their leader, either in his good or in his evil fortunes. This we can only ascribe to the transcendent cruelty, which, joined with numberless great qualities, rendered him at once venerable and terrible in the eyes of his soldiers; for without this reputation for cruelty these other virtues would not have produced the like results.

Unreflecting writers, indeed, while they praise his achievements, have condemned the chief cause of them; but that his other merits would not by themselves have been so efficacious we may see from the case of Scipio, one of the greatest Captains, not of his own time only but of all times of which we have record, whose armies rose against him in Spain from no other cause than his too great leniency in allowing them a freedom inconsistent with military strictness. With which weakness Fabius Maximus taxed him in the Senate House, calling him the corrupter of the Roman soldiery. Again, when the Locrians were shamefully outraged by one of his lieutenants, he neither avenged them, nor punished the insolence of his officer; and this from the natural easiness of his disposition. So that it was said in the Senate by one who sought to excuse him, that there were many who knew better how to refrain from doing wrong themselves than how to correct the wrong-doing of others. This temper, however, must in time have marred the name and fame even of Scipio, had he continued in it, and retained his command. But living as he did under the control of the Senate, this hurtful quality was not merely disguised, but came to be regarded as a glory.

Returning to the question of being loved or feared, I sum up by saying, that since his being loved depends upon his subjects, while his being feared depends upon himself, a wise Prince should build on what is his own, and not on what rests with others. Only, as I have said, he must do his utmost to escape hatred.

Chapter XVIII.

How Princes Should Keep Faith

Everyone understands how praiseworthy it is in a Prince to keep faith, and to live uprightly and not craftily. Nevertheless, we see from what has taken place in our own days that Princes who have set little store by their word, but have known how to overreach men by their cunning, have accomplished great things, and in the end got the better of those who trusted to honest dealing.

Be it known, then, that there are two ways of contending, one in accordance with the laws, the other by force; the first of which is proper to men, the second to beasts. But since the first method is often ineffectual, it becomes necessary to resort to the second. A Prince should, therefore, understand how to use well both the man and the beast. And this lesson has been covertly taught by the ancient writers, who relate how Achilles and many others of these old Princes were given over to be brought up and trained by Chiron the Centaur; since the only meaning of their having for instructor one who was half man and half beast is, that it is necessary for a Prince to know how to use both natures, and that the one without the other has no stability.

But since a Prince should know how to use the beast's nature wisely, he ought of beasts to choose both the lion and the fox; for the lion cannot guard himself from the toils, nor the fox from wolves. He must therefore be a fox to discern toils, and a lion to drive off wolves.

To rely wholly on the lion is unwise; and for this reason a prudent Prince neither can nor ought to keep his word when to keep it is hurtful to him and the causes which led him to pledge it are removed. If all men were good, this would not be good advice, but since they are dishonest and do not keep faith with you, you in return, need not keep faith with them; and no prince was ever at a loss for plausible reasons to cloak a breach of faith. Of this numberless recent instances could be given, and it might be shown how many solemn treaties and engagements have been rendered inoperative and idle through want of faith in Princes, and that he who was best known to play the fox has had the best success.

It is necessary, indeed, to put a good colour on this nature, and to be skillful in simulating and dissembling. But men are so simple, and governed so absolutely by their present needs, that he who wishes to deceive will never fail in finding willing dupes. One recent example I will not omit. Pope Alexander VI had no care or thought but how to deceive, and always found material to work on. No man ever had a more effective manner of asseverating, or made promises with more solemn protestations, or observed them less. And yet, because he understood this side of human nature, his frauds always succeeded.

It is not essential, then, that a Prince should have all the good qualities which I have enumerated above, but it is most essential that he should seem to have them; I will even venture to affirm that if he has and invariably practises them all, they are hurtful, whereas the appearance of having them is useful. Thus, it is well to seem merciful, faithful, humane, religious, and upright, and also to be so; but the mind should remain so balanced that were it needful not to be so, you should be able and know how to change to the contrary.

And you are to understand that a Prince, and most of all a new Prince, cannot observe all those rules of conduct in respect whereof men are accounted good, being often forced, in order to preserve his Princedom, to act in opposition to good faith, charity, humanity, and religion. He must therefore keep his mind ready to shift as the winds and tides of Fortune turn, and, as I have already said, he ought not to quit good courses if he can help it, but should know how to follow evil courses if he must.

A Prince should therefore be very careful that nothing ever escapes his lips which is not replete with the five qualities above named, so that to see and hear him, one would think him the embodiment of mercy, good faith, integrity, humanity, and religion. And there is no virtue which it is more necessary for him to seem to possess than this last; because men in general judge rather by the eye than by the hand, for every one can see but few can touch. Everyone sees what you seem, but few know what you are, and these few dare not oppose themselves to the opinion of the many who have the majesty of the State to back them up.

Moreover, in the actions of all men, and most of all of Princes, where there is no tribunal to which we can appeal, we look to results. Wherefore if a Prince succeeds in establishing and maintaining his authority, the means will always be judged honourable and be approved by everyone. For the vulgar are always taken by appearances and by results, and the world is made up of the vulgar, the few only finding room when the many have no longer ground to stand on.

A certain Prince of our own days, whose name it is as well not to mention, is always preaching peace and good faith, although the mortal enemy of both; and both, had he practised them as he preaches them, would, oftener than once, have lost him his kingdom and authority.

Chapter XIX.

That a Prince Should Seek to Escape Contempt and Hatred

Having now spoken of the chief of the qualities above referred to, the rest I shall dispose of briefly with these general remarks, that a Prince, as has already in part been said, should consider how he may avoid such courses as would make him hated or despised; and that whenever he succeeds in keeping clear of these, he has performed his part, and runs no risk though he incur other infamies.

A Prince, as I have said before, sooner becomes hated by being rapacious and by interfering with the property and with the women of his subjects, than in any other way. From these, therefore, he should abstain. For so long as neither their property nor their honour is touched, the mass of mankind live contentedly, and the Prince has only to cope with the ambition of a few, which can in many ways and easily be kept within bounds.

A Prince is despised when he is seen to be fickle, frivolous, effeminate, pusillanimous, or irresolute, against which defects he ought therefore most carefully to guard, striving so to bear himself that greatness, courage, wisdom, and strength may appear in all his actions. In his private dealings with his subjects his decisions should be irrevocable, and his reputation such that no one would dream of overreaching or cajoling him.

The Prince who inspires such an opinion of himself is greatly esteemed, and against one who is greatly esteemed conspiracy is difficult; nor, when he is known to be an excellent Prince and held in reverence by his subjects, will it be easy to attack him. For a Prince is exposed to two dangers, from within in respect of his subjects, from without in respect of foreign powers. Against the latter he will defend himself with good arms and good allies, and if he have good arms he will always have good allies; and when things are settled abroad, they will always be settled at home, unless disturbed by conspiracies; and even should there be hostility from without, if he has taken those measures, and has lived in the way I have recommended, and if he never abandons hope, he will withstand every attack; as I have said was done by Nabis the Spartan.

As regards his own subjects, when affairs are quiet abroad, he has to fear they may engage in secret plots; against which a Prince best secures himself when he escapes being hated or despised, and keeps on good terms with his people; and this, as I have already shown at length, it is essential he should do. Not to be hated or despised by the body of his subjects, is one of the surest safeguards that a Prince can have against conspiracy. For he who conspires always reckons on pleasing the people by putting the Prince to death; but when he sees that instead of pleasing he will offend them, he cannot summon courage to carry out his design. For the difficulties that attend conspirators are infinite, and we know from experience that while there have been many conspiracies, few of them have succeeded.

He who conspires cannot do so alone, nor can he assume as his companions any save those whom he believes to be discontented; but so soon as you impart your design to a discontented man, you supply him with the means of removing his discontent, since by betraying you he can procure for himself every advantage; so that seeing on the one hand certain gain, and on the other a doubtful and dangerous risk, he must either be a rare friend to you, or the mortal enemy of his Prince, if he keep your secret.

To put the matter shortly, I say that on the side of the conspirator there are distrust, jealousy, and dread of punishment to deter him, while on the side of the Prince there are the laws, the majesty of the throne, the protection of friends and of the government to defend him; to which if the general good-will of the people be added, it is hardly possible that any should be rash enough to conspire. For while in ordinary cases, the conspirator has ground for fear only before the execution of his villainy, in this case he has also cause to fear after the crime has been perpetrated, since he has the people for his enemy, and is thus cut off from every hope of shelter.

Of this, endless instances might be given, but I shall content myself with one that happened within the recollection of our fathers. Messer Annibale Bentivoglio, Lord of Bologna and grandfather of the present Messer Annibale, was conspired against and murdered by the

Canneschi, leaving behind none belonging to him save Messer Giovanni, then an infant in arms. Immediately upon the murder, the people rose and put all the Canneschi to death. This resulted from the general goodwill with which the House of the Bentivogli was then regarded in Bologna; which feeling was so strong, that when upon the death of Messer Annibale no one was left who could govern the State, there being reason to believe that a descendant of the family (who up to that time had been thought to be the son of a smith), was living in Florence, the citizens of Bologna came there for him, and entrusted him with the government of their city; which he retained until Messer Giovanni was old enough to govern.

To be brief, a Prince has little to fear from conspiracies when his subjects are well disposed towards him; but when they are hostile and hold him in detestation, he has then reason to fear everything and everyone. And well-ordered States and wise Princes have provided with extreme care that the nobility shall not be driven to desperation, and that the commons shall be kept satisfied and contented; for this is one of the most important matters that a Prince has to look to.

Among the well-ordered and governed Kingdoms of our day is that of France, wherein we find an infinite number of wise institutions, upon which depend the freedom and the security of the King, and of which the most important are the Parliament and its authority. For he who gave its constitution to this Realm, knowing the ambition and arrogance of the nobles, and judging it necessary to bridle and restrain them, and on the other hand knowing the hatred, originating in fear, entertained against them by the commons, and desiring that they should be safe, was unwilling that the responsibility for this should rest on the King; and to relieve him of the ill-will which he might incur with the nobles by favouring the commons, or with the commons by favouring the nobles, appointed a third party to be arbitrator, who without committing the King, might depress the nobles and uphold the commons. Nor could there be any better, wiser, or surer safeguard for the King and the Kingdom. And hence we may draw another notable lesson, namely, that Princes should devolve on others those matters that entail responsibility, and reserve to themselves those that relate to grace and favour. And again I say that a Prince should esteem the great, but must not make himself odious to the people.

To some it may perhaps appear, that if the lives and deaths of many of the Roman Emperors be considered, they offer examples opposed to the views expressed by me; since we find that some among them who had always lived good lives, and shown themselves possessed of great qualities, were nevertheless deposed and even put to death by their subjects who had conspired against them.

In answer to such objections, I shall examine the characters of several Emperors, and show that the causes of their downfall were in no way different from those which I have indicated. In doing this I shall submit for consideration such matters only as must strike everyone who reads the history of these times; and it will be enough for my purpose to take those Emperors who reigned from the time of Marcus the Philosopher to the time of Maximinus, who were, inclusively, Marcus, Commodus his son, Pertinax, Julianus, Severus, Caracalla his son, Macrinus, Heliogabalus, Alexander, and Maximinus.

In the first place, then, we have to note that while in other Princedoms the Prince has only to contend with the ambition of the nobles and the insubordination of the people, the Roman Emperors had a further difficulty to encounter in the cruelty and rapacity of their soldiers, which were so distracting as to cause the ruin of many of these Princes. For it was hardly possible for them to satisfy both the soldiers and the people; the latter loving peace and therefore preferring sober Princes, while the former preferred a Prince of a warlike spirit, however harsh, haughty, or rapacious; being willing that he should exercise these qualities against the people, as the means of procuring for themselves double pay, and indulging their greed and cruelty.

Whence it followed that those Emperors who had not inherited or won for themselves such authority as enabled them to keep both people and soldiers in check, were always ruined. The most of them, and those especially who came to the Empire new and without experience, seeing the difficulty of dealing with these conflicting humours, set themselves to satisfy the soldiers, and made little account of offending the people. And for them this was a necessary course to take; for as Princes cannot escape being hated by some, they should, in the first place, endeavour not to be hated by a class; failing in which, they must do all they can to escape the hatred of that class which is the stronger. Wherefore those Emperors who, by reason of their newness, stood in need of extraordinary support, sided with the soldiery rather than with the people; a course which turned out advantageous or otherwise, according as the Prince knew, or did not know, how to maintain his authority over them.

From the causes indicated it resulted that Marcus, Pertinax, and Alexander, being Princes of a temperate disposition, lovers of justice, enemies of cruelty, gentle, and kindly, had all, save Marcus, an unhappy end. Marcus alone lived and died honoured in the highest degree; and this because he had succeeded to the Empire by right of inheritance, and not through the favour either of the soldiery or of the people; and also because, being endowed with many virtues which made him revered, he kept, while he lived, both factions within bounds, and was never either hated or despised.

But Pertinax was chosen Emperor against the will of the soldiery, who being accustomed to a licentious life under Commodus, could not tolerate the stricter discipline to which his successor sought to bring them back. And having thus made himself hated, and being at the same time despised by reason of his advanced age, he was ruined at the very outset of his reign.

And here it is to be noted that hatred is incurred as well on account of good actions as of bad; or which reason, as I have already said, a Prince who would maintain his authority is often compelled to be other than good. For when the class, be it the people, the soldiers, or the nobles, on whom you judge it necessary to rely for your support, is corrupt, you must needs adapt yourself to its humours, and satisfy these, in which case virtuous conduct will only prejudice you.

Let us now come to Alexander, who was so just a ruler that among the praises ascribed to him it is recorded, that, during the fourteen years he held the Empire, no man was ever put to death by him without trial. Nevertheless, being accounted effeminate, and thought to be governed by his mother, he fell into contempt, and the army conspiring against him, slew him.

When we turn to consider the characters of Commodus, Severus, and Caracalla, we find them all to have been most cruel and rapacious Princes, who to satisfy the soldiery, scrupled not to inflict every kind of wrong upon the people. And all of them, except Severus, came to a bad end. But in Severus there was such strength of character, that, keeping the soldiers his friends, he was able, although he oppressed the people, to reign on prosperously to the last; because his great qualities made him so admirable in the eyes both of the people and the soldiers, that the former remained in a manner amazed and awestruck, while the latter were respectful and contented.

And because his actions, for one who was a new Prince, were thus remarkable, I will point out shortly how well he understood to play the part both of the lion and of the fox, each of which natures, as I have observed before, a Prince should know how to assume.

Knowing the indolent disposition of the Emperor Julianus, Severus persuaded the army which he commanded in Illyria that it was their duty to go to Rome to avenge the death of Pertinax, who had been slain by the Pretorian guards. Under this pretext, and without disclosing his design on the Empire, he put his army in march, and reached Italy before it was known that he had set out. On his arrival in Rome, the Senate, through fear, elected him Emperor and put Julianus to death. After taking this first step, two obstacles still remained to his becoming sole master of the Empire; one in Asia, where Niger who commanded the armies of the East had caused himself to be proclaimed Emperor; the other in the West, where Albinus, who also aspired to the Empire, was in command. And as Severus judged it dangerous to declare open war against both, he resolved to proceed against Niger by arms, and against Albinus by artifice. To the latter, accordingly, he wrote, that having been chosen Emperor by the Senate, he desired to share the dignity with him; that he therefore sent him the title of Caesar, and in accordance with a resolution of the Senate assumed him as his colleague. All which statements Albinus accepted as true. But so soon as Severus had defeated and slain Niger, and restored tranquillity in the East, returning to Rome he complained in the Senate that Albinus, all unmindful of the favours he had received from him, had treacherously sought to destroy him; for which cause he was compelled to go and punish his ingratitude. Whereupon he set forth to seek Albinus in Gaul, where he at once deprived him of his dignities and his life.

Whoever, therefore, examines carefully the actions of this Emperor, will find in him all the fierceness of the lion and all the craft of the fox, and will note how he was feared and respected by the people, yet not hated by the army, and will not be surprised that though a new man, he was able to maintain his hold of so great an Empire. For the splendour of his reputation always shielded him from the odium which the people might otherwise have conceived against him by reason of his cruelty and rapacity.

Caracalla, his son, was likewise a man of great parts, endowed with qualities that made him admirable in the sight of the people, and endeared him to the army, being of a warlike spirit, most patient of fatigue, and contemning all luxury in food and every other effeminacy. Nevertheless, his ferocity and cruelty were so extravagant and unheard of (he having put to death a vast number of the inhabitants of Rome at different times, and the whole of those of Alexandria at a stroke), that he came to be detested by all the world, and so feared even by those whom he had about him, that at the last he was slain by a centurion in the midst of his army.

And here let it be noted that deaths like this which are the result of a deliberate and fixed resolve, cannot be escaped by Princes, since anyone who disregards his own life can effect them. A Prince, however, needs the less to fear them as they are seldom attempted. The only precaution he can take is to avoid doing grave wrong to any of those who serve him, or whom he has near him as officers of his Court, a precaution which Caracalla neglected in putting to a shameful death the brother of this centurion, and in using daily threats against the man himself, whom he nevertheless retained as one of his bodyguard. This, as the event showed, was a rash and fatal course.

We come next to Commodus, who, as he took the Empire by hereditary right, ought to have held it with much ease. For being the son of Marcus, he had only to follow in his father's footsteps to content both the people and the soldiery. But being of a cruel and brutal nature, to sate his rapacity at the expense of the people, he sought support from the army, and indulged it in every kind of excess. On the other hand, by an utter disregard of his dignity, in frequently descending into the arena to fight with gladiators, and by other base acts wholly unworthy of the

Imperial station, he became contemptible in the eyes of the soldiery; and being on the one hand hated, on the other despised, was at last conspired against and murdered.

The character of Maximinus remains to be touched upon. He was of a very warlike disposition, and on the death of Alexander, of whom we have already spoken, was chosen Emperor by the army who had been displeased with the effeminacy of that Prince. But this dignity he did not long enjoy, since two causes concurred to render him at once odious and contemptible; the one the baseness of his origin, he having at one time herded sheep in Thrace, a fact well known to all, and which led all to look on him with disdain; the other that on being proclaimed Emperor, delaying to repair to Rome and enter on possession of the Imperial throne, he incurred the reputation of excessive cruelty by reason of the many atrocities perpetrated by his prefects in Rome and other parts of the Empire. The result was that the whole world, stirred at once with scorn of his mean birth and with the hatred which the dread of his ferocity inspired, combined against him, Africa leading the way, the Senate and people of Rome and the whole of Italy following. In which conspiracy his own army joined. For they, being engaged in the siege of Aquileja and finding difficulty in reducing it, disgusted with his cruelty, and less afraid of him when they saw so many against him, put him to death.

I need say nothing of Heliogabalus, Macrinus, or Julianus, all of whom being utterly despicable, came to a speedy downfall, but shall conclude these remarks by observing, that the Princes of our own days are less troubled with the difficulty of having to make constant efforts to keep their soldier in good humour. For though they must treat them with some indulgence, the need for doing so is soon over, since none of these Princes possesses a standing army which, like the armies of the Roman Empire, has strengthened with the growth of his government and the administration of his State. And if it was then necessary to satisfy the soldiers rather than the people, because the soldiers were more powerful than the people, now it is more necessary for all Princes, except the Turk and the Soldan, to satisfy the people rather than the soldiery, since the former are more powerful than the latter.

I except the Turk because he has always about him some twelve thousand foot soldiers and fifteen thousand horse, on whom depend the security and strength of his kingdom, and with whom he must needs keep on good terms, all regard for the people being subordinate. The government of the Soldan is similar, so that he too being wholly in the hands of his soldiers, must keep well with them without regard to the people.

And here you are to note that the State of the Soldan, while it is unlike all other Princedoms, resembles the Christian Pontificate in this, that it can neither be classed as new, nor as hereditary. For the sons of a

Soldan who dies do not succeed to the kingdom as his heirs, but he who is elected to the post by those who have authority to make such elections. And this being the ancient and established order of things, the Princedoms cannot be accounted new, since none of the difficulties that attend new Princedoms are found in it. For although the Prince be new, the institutions of the State are old, and are so contrived that the elected Prince is accepted as though he were an hereditary Sovereign.

But returning to the matter in hand, I say that whoever reflects on the above reasoning will see that either hatred or contempt was the ruin of the Emperors whom I have named; and will also understand how it happened that some taking one way and some the opposite, one only by each of these roads came to a happy, and all the rest to an unhappy end. Because for Pertinax and Alexander, they being new Princes, it was useless and hurtful to try to imitate Marcus, who was an hereditary Prince; and similarly for Caracalla, Commodus, and Maximinus it was a fatal error to imitate Severus, since they lacked the qualities that would have enabled them to tread in his footsteps.

In short, a Prince new to the Princedom cannot imitate the actions of Marcus, nor is it necessary that he should imitate all those of Severus; but he should borrow from Severus those parts of his conduct which are needed to serve as a foundation for his government, and from Marcus those suited to maintain it, and render it glorious when once established.

Chapter XX.

Whether Fortresses, and Certain Other Expedients to Which Princes Often Have Recourse, are Profitable or Hurtful

To govern more securely some Princes have disarmed their subjects, others have kept the towns subject to them divided by factions; some have fostered hostility against themselves, others have sought to gain over those who at the beginning of their reign were looked on with suspicion; some have built fortresses, others have dismantled and destroyed them; and though no definite judgment can be pronounced respecting any of these methods, without regard to the special circumstances of the State to which it is proposed to apply them, I shall nevertheless speak of them in as comprehensive a way as the nature of the subject will admit.

It has never chanced that any new Prince has disarmed his subjects. On the contrary, when he has found them unarmed he has always armed them. For the arms thus provided become yours, those whom you suspected grow faithful, while those who were faithful at the first, continue so, and from your subjects become your partisans. And though all your subjects cannot be armed, yet if those of them whom you arm be treated with marked favour, you can deal more securely with the rest. For the difference which those whom you supply with arms perceive in their treatment, will bind them to you, while the others will excuse you, recognizing that those who incur greater risk and responsibility merit greater rewards. But by disarming, you at once give offence, since you show your subjects that you distrust them, either as doubting their courage, or as doubting their fidelity, each of which imputations begets hatred against you. Moreover, as you cannot maintain yourself without arms you must have recourse to mercenary troops. What these are I have already shown, but even if they were good, they could never avail to defend you, at once against powerful enemies abroad and against subjects whom you distrust. Wherefore, as I have said already, new Princes in new Princedoms have always provided for their being armed; and of instances of this History is full.

But when a Prince acquires a new State, which thus becomes joined on like a limb to his old possessions, he must disarm its inhabitants, except such of them as have taken part with him while he was acquiring it; and even these, as time and occasion serve, he should seek to render soft and effeminate; and he must so manage matters that all the arms of the new State shall be in the hands of his own soldiers who have served under him in his ancient dominions.

Our forefathers, even such among them as were esteemed wise, were wont to say that '*Pistoia was to be held by feuds, and Pisa by fortresses,*' and on this principle used to promote dissensions in various subject towns with a view to retain them with less effort. At a time when Italy was in some measure in equilibrium, this may have been a prudent course to follow; but at the present day it seems impossible to recommend it as a general rule of policy. For I do not believe that divisions purposely caused can ever lead to good; on the contrary, when an enemy approaches, divided cities are lost at once, for the weaker faction will always side with the invader, and the other will not be able to stand alone.

The Venetians, influenced as I believe by the reasons above mentioned, fostered the factions of Guelf and Ghibelline in the cities subject to them; and though they did not suffer blood to be shed, fomented their feuds, in order that the citizens having their minds occupied with these disputes might not conspire against them. But this, as we know, did not turn out to their advantage, for after their defeat at Vaila, one of the two factions, suddenly taking courage, deprived them of the whole of their territory.

Moreover methods like these argue weakness in a Prince, for under a strong government such divisions would never be permitted, since they are profitable only in time of peace as an expedient whereby subjects may be more easily managed; but when war breaks out their insufficiency is demonstrated.

Doubtless, Princes become great by vanquishing difficulties and opposition, and Fortune, on that account, when she desires to aggrandize a new Prince, who has more need than an hereditary Prince to win reputation, causes enemies to spring up, and urges them on to attack him, to the end that he may have opportunities to overcome them, and make his ascent by the very ladder which they have planted. For which reason, many are of the opinion that a wise Prince, when he has the occasion, ought dexterously to promote hostility to himself in certain quarters, in order that his greatness may be enhanced by crushing it.

Princes, and new Princes especially, have found greater fidelity and helpfulness in those whom, at the beginning of their reign, they have held in suspicion, than in those who at the outset have enjoyed their confidence; and Pandolfo Petrucci, Lord of Siena, governed his State by the instrumentality of those whom he had at one time distrusted, in preference to all others. But on this point it is impossible to lay down any general rule, since the course to be followed varies with the circumstances. This only I will say, that those men who at the beginning of a reign have been hostile, if of a sort requiring support to maintain them, may always be won over by the Prince with much ease, and are the more bound to serve him faithfully because they know that they have to efface by their conduct the unfavourable impression he had formed of them; and in this way a Prince always obtains better help from them, than from those who serving him in too complete security neglect his affairs.

And since the subject suggests it, I must not fail to remind the Prince who acquires a new State through the favour of its inhabitants, to weigh well what were the causes which led those who favoured him to do so; and if it be seen that they have acted not from any natural affection for him, but merely out of discontent with the former government, that he will find the greatest difficulty in keeping them his friends, since it will be impossible for him to content them. Carefully considering the cause of this, with the aid of examples taken from times ancient and modern, he will perceive that it is far easier to secure the friendship of those who being satisfied with things as they stood, were for that very reason his enemies, than of those who sided with him and aided him in his usurpation only because they were discontented.

It has been customary for Princes, with a view to hold their dominions more securely, to build fortresses which might serve as a curb and restraint on such as have designs against them, and as a safe refuge against a first onset. I approve this custom, because it has been followed from the earliest times. Nevertheless, in our own days, Messer Niccolò Vitelli thought it prudent to dismantle two fortresses in Città di Castello in order to secure that town: and Guido Ubaldo, Duke of Urbino, on returning to his dominions, whence he had been driven by

Cesare Borgia, razed to their foundations the fortresses throughout the Dukedom, judging that if these were removed, it would not again be so easily lost. A like course was followed by the Bentivogli on their return to Bologna.

Fortresses, therefore, are useful or no, according to circumstances, and if in one way they benefit, in another they injure you. We may state the case thus: the Prince who is more afraid of his subjects than of strangers ought to build fortresses, while he who is more afraid of strangers than of his subjects, should leave them alone. The citadel built by Francesco Sforza in Milan, has been, and will hereafter prove to be, more dangerous to the House of Sforza than any other disorder of that State. So that, on the whole, the best fortress you can have, is in not being hated by your subjects. If they hate you no fortress will save you; for when once the people take up arms, foreigners are never wanting to assist them.

Within our own time it does not appear that fortresses have been of service to any Prince, unless to the Countess of Forli after her husband Count Girolamo was murdered; for by this means she was able to escape the first onset of the insurgents, and awaiting succour from Milan, to recover her State; the circumstances of the times not allowing any foreigner to lend assistance to the people. But afterwards, when she was attacked by Cesare Borgia, and the people, out of hostility to her, took part with the invader, her fortresses were of little avail. So that, both on this and on the former occasion, it would have been safer for her to have had no fortresses, than to have had her subjects for enemies.

All which considerations taken into account, I shall applaud him who builds fortresses, and him who does not; but I shall blame him who, trusting in them, reckons it a light thing to be held in hatred by his people.

Chapter XXI.

How a Prince Should Bear Himself So As to Acquire Reputation

Nothing makes a Prince so well thought of as to undertake great enterprises and give striking proofs of his capacity.

Among the Princes of our time Ferdinand of Aragon, the present King of Spain, may almost be accounted a new Prince, since from one of the weakest he has become, for fame and glory, the foremost King in Christendom. And if you consider his achievements you will find them all great and some extraordinary.

In the beginning of his reign he made war on Granada, which enterprise was the foundation of his power. At first he carried on the war leisurely, without fear of interruption, and kept the attention and thoughts of the Barons of Castile so completely occupied with it, that they had no time to think of changes at home. Meanwhile he insensibly acquired reputation among them and authority over them. With the money of the Church and of his subjects he was able to maintain his armies, and during the prolonged contest to lay the foundations of that military discipline which afterwards made him so famous. Moreover, to enable him to engage in still greater undertakings, always covering himself with the cloak of religion, he had recourse to what may be called *pious cruelty*, in driving out and clearing his Kingdom of the Moors; than which exploit none could be more wonderful or uncommon. Using the same pretext he made war on Africa, invaded Italy, and finally attacked France; and being thus constantly busied in planning and executing vast designs, he kept the minds of his subjects in suspense and admiration, and occupied with the results of his actions, which arose one out of another in such close succession as left neither time nor opportunity to oppose them.

Again, it greatly profits a Prince in conducting the internal government of his State, to follow striking methods, such as are recorded of Messer Bernabò of Milan, whenever the remarkable actions of any one in civil life, whether for good or for evil, afford him occasion; and to choose such ways of rewarding and punishing as cannot fail to be much spoken of. But above all, he should strive by all his actions to inspire a sense of his greatness and goodness.

A Prince is likewise esteemed who is a stanch friend and a thorough foe, that is to say, who without reserve openly declares for one against another, this being always a more advantageous course than to stand neutral. For supposing two of your powerful neighbours come to blows, it must either be that you have, or have not, reason to fear the one who comes off victorious. In either case it will always be well for you to declare yourself, and join in frankly with one side or other. For should you fail to do so you are certain, in the former of the cases put, to become the prey of the victor to the satisfaction and delight of the vanquished, and no reason or circumstance that you may plead will avail to shield or shelter you; for the victor dislikes doubtful friends, and such as will not help him at a pinch; and the vanquished will have nothing to say to you, since you would not share his fortunes sword in hand.

When Antiochus, at the instance of the Aetolians, passed into Greece in order to drive out the Romans, he sent envoys to the Achaians, who were friendly to the Romans, exhorting them to stand neutral. The Romans, on the other hand, urged them to take up arms on their behalf. The matter coming to be discussed in the Council of the Achaians, the legate of Antiochus again urged neutrality, whereupon the Roman envoy answered—'Nothing can be less to your advantage than the course which has been recommended as the best and most useful for your State, namely, to refrain from taking any part in our war, for by standing aloof you will gain neither favour nor fame, but remain the prize of the victor.' And it will always happen that he who is not your friend will invite you to neutrality, while he who is your friend will call on you to declare yourself openly in arms. Irresolute Princes, to escape immediate danger, commonly follow the neutral path, in most instances to their destruction. But when you pronounce valiantly in favour of one side or other, if he to whom you give your adherence conquers, although he be powerful and you are at his mercy, still he is under obligations to you, and has become your friend; and none are so lost to shame as to destroy with manifest ingratitude, one who has helped them. Besides which, victories are never so complete that the victor can afford to disregard all considerations whatsoever, more especially considerations of justice. On the other hand, if he with whom you take part should lose, you will always be favourably regarded by him; while he can he will aid you, and you become his companion in a cause which may recover.

In the second case, namely, when both combatants are of such limited strength that whichever wins you have no cause to fear, it is all the more prudent for you to take a side, for you will then be ruining the one with the help of the other, who were he wise would endeavour to save him. If he whom you help conquers, he remains in your power, and with your aid he cannot but conquer.

And here let it be noted that a Prince should be careful never to join with one stronger than himself in attacking others, unless, as already said, he be driven to it by necessity. For if he whom you join prevails, you are at his mercy; and Princes, so far as in them lies, should avoid placing themselves at the mercy of others. The Venetians, although they might have declined the alliance, joined with France against the Duke of Milan, which brought about their ruin. But when an alliance cannot be avoided, as was the case with the Florentines when the Pope and Spain together led their armies to attack Lombardy, a Prince, for the reasons given, must take a side. Nor let it be supposed that any State can choose for itself a perfectly safe line of policy. On the contrary, it must reckon on every course which it may take being doubtful; for it happens in all human affairs that we never seek to escape one mischief without falling into another. Prudence therefore consists in knowing how to distinguish degrees of disadvantage, and in accepting a less evil as a good.

Again, a Prince should show himself a patron of merit, and should honour those who excel in every art. He ought accordingly to encourage his subjects by enabling them to pursue their callings, whether mercantile, agricultural, or any other, in security, so that this man shall not be deterred from beautifying his possessions from the apprehension that they may be taken from him, or that other refrain from opening a trade through fear of taxes; and he should provide rewards for those who desire so to employ themselves, and for all who are disposed in any way to add to the greatness of his City or State.

He ought, moreover, at suitable seasons of the year to entertain the people with festivals and shows. And because all cities are divided into guilds and companies, he should show attention to these societies, and sometimes take part in their meetings; offering an example of courtesy and munificence, but always maintaining the dignity of his station, which must under no circumstances be compromised.

Chapter XXII.

Of the Secretaries of Princes

The choice of Ministers is a matter of no small moment to a Prince. Whether they shall be good or no depends on his prudence, so that the readiest conjecture we can form of the character and sagacity of a Prince, is from seeing what sort of men he has about him. When they are at once capable and faithful, we may always account him wise, since he has known to recognize their merit and to retain their fidelity. But if they be otherwise, we must pronounce unfavourably of him, since he has committed a first fault in making this selection.

There was none who knew Messer Antonio of Venafro, as Minister of Pandolfo Petrucci, Lord of Siena, but thought Pandolfo a most prudent ruler in having him for his servant. And since there are three scales of intelligence, one which understands by itself, a second which understands what is shown it by others, and a third which understands neither by itself nor on the showing of others, the first of which is most excellent, the second good, but the third worthless, we must needs admit that if Pandolfo was not in the first of these degrees, he was in the second; for when one has the judgment to discern the good from the bad in what another says or does, though he be devoid of invention, he can recognize the merits and demerits of his servant, and will commend the former while he corrects the latter. The servant cannot hope to deceive such a master, and will continue good.

As to how a Prince is to know his Minister, this unerring rule may be laid down. When you see a Minister thinking more of himself than of you, and in all his actions seeking his own ends, that man can never be a good Minister or one that you can trust. For he who has the charge of the State committed to him, ought not to think of himself, but only of his Prince, and should never bring to the notice of the latter what does not directly concern him. On the other hand, to keep his Minister good, the Prince should be considerate of him, dignifying him, enriching him, binding him to himself by benefits, and sharing with him the honours as well as the burthens of the State, so that the abundant honours and wealth bestowed upon him may divert him from seeking them at other hands; while the great responsibilities wherewith he is charged may lead him to dread change, knowing that he cannot stand alone without his master's support. When Prince and Minister are upon this footing they can mutually trust one another; but when the contrary is the case, it will always fare ill with one or other of them.

Chapter XXIII.

That Flatterers Should Be Shunned

One error into which Princes, unless very prudent or very fortunate in their choice of friends, are apt to fall, is of so great importance that I must not pass it over. I mean in respect of flatterers. These abound in Courts, because men take such pleasure in their own concerns, and so deceive themselves with regard to them, that they can hardly escape this plague; while even in the effort to escape it there is risk of their incurring contempt.

For there is no way to guard against flattery but by letting it be seen that you take no offense in hearing the truth: but when everyone is free to tell you the truth respect falls short. Wherefore a prudent Prince should follow a middle course, by choosing certain discreet men from among his subjects, and allowing them alone free leave to speak their minds on any matter on which he asks their opinion, and on none other. But he ought to ask their opinion on everything, and after hearing what they have to say, should reflect and judge for himself. And with these counsellors collectively, and with each of them separately, his bearing should be such, that each and all of them may know that the more freely they declare their thoughts the better they will be liked. Besides these, the Prince should hearken to no others, but should follow the course determined on, and afterwards adhere firmly to his resolves. Whoever acts otherwise is either undone by flatterers, or from continually vacillating as opinions vary, comes to be held in light esteem.

With reference to this matter, I shall cite a recent instance. Father Luke, who is attached to the Court of the present Emperor Maximilian, in speaking of his Majesty told me, that he seeks advice from none, yet never has his own way; and this from his following a course contrary to that above recommended. For being of a secret disposition, he never discloses his intentions to any, nor asks their opinion; and it is only when his plans are to be carried out that they begin to be discovered and known, and at the same time they begin to be thwarted by those he has about him, when he being facile gives way. Hence it happens that what he does one day, he undoes the next; that his wishes and designs are never fully ascertained; and that it is impossible to build on his resolves.

A Prince, therefore, ought always to take counsel, but at such times and reasons only as he himself pleases, and not when it pleases others; nay, he should discourage everyone from obtruding advice on matters on which it is not sought. But he should be free in asking advice, and afterwards as regards the matters on which he has asked it, a patient hearer of the truth, and even displeased should he perceive that any one, from whatever motive, keeps it back.

But those who think that every Prince who has a name for prudence owes it to the wise counsellors he has around him, and not to any merit of his own, are certainly mistaken; since it is an unerring rule and of universal application that a Prince who is not wise himself cannot be well advised by others, unless by chance he surrender himself to be wholly governed by someone adviser who happens to be supremely prudent; in which case he may, indeed, be well advised; but not for long, since such an adviser will soon deprive him of his Government. If he listen to a multitude of advisers, the Prince who is not wise will never have consistent counsels, nor will he know of himself how to reconcile them. Each of his counsellors will study his own advantage, and the Prince will be unable to detect or correct them. Nor could it well be otherwise, for men will always grow rogues on your hands unless they find themselves under a necessity to be honest.

Hence it follows that good counsels, whencesoever they come, have their origin in the prudence of the Prince, and not the prudence of the Prince in wise counsels.

Chapter XXIV.

Why the Princes of Italy Have Lost Their States

The lessons above taught if prudently followed will make a new Prince seem like an old one, and will soon seat him in his place more firmly and securely than if his authority had the sanction of time. For the actions of a new Prince are watched much more closely than those of an hereditary Prince; and when seen to be good are far more effectual than antiquity of blood in gaining men over and attaching them to his cause. For men are more nearly touched by things present than by things past, and when they find themselves well off as they are, enjoy their felicity and seek no further; nay, are ready to do their utmost in defence of the new Prince, provided he be not wanting to himself in other respects. In this way there accrues to him a twofold glory, in having laid the foundations of the new Princedom, and in having strengthened and adorned it with good laws and good arms, with faithful friends and great deeds; as, on the other hand, there is a double disgrace in one who has been born to a Princedom losing it by his own want of wisdom.

And if we contemplate those Lords who in our own times have lost their dominions in Italy, such as the King of Naples, the Duke of Milan, and others, in the first place we shall see, that in respect of arms they have, for reasons already dwelt on, been all alike defective; and next, that some of them have either had the people against them, or if they have had the people with them, have not known how to secure themselves against their nobles. For without such defects as these, States powerful enough to keep an army in the field are never overthrown.

Philip of Macedon, not the father of Alexander the Great, but he who was vanquished by Titus Quintius, had no great State as compared with the strength of the Romans and Greeks who attacked him. Nevertheless, being a Prince of a warlike spirit, and skillful in gaining the good will of the people and in securing the fidelity of the nobles, he maintained himself for many years against his assailants, and in the end, though he lost some towns, succeeded in saving his Kingdom.

Let those Princes of ours, therefore, who, after holding them for a length of years, have lost their dominions, blame not Fortune but their own inertness. For never having reflected in tranquil times that there might come a change (and it is human nature when the sea is calm not to think of storms), when adversity overtook them, they thought not of defence but only of escape, hoping that their people, disgusted with the arrogance of the conqueror, would someday recall them.

This course may be a good one to follow when all others fail, but it were the height of folly, trusting to it, to abandon every other; since none would wish to fall on the chance of someone else being found to lift him up. It may not happen that you are recalled by your people, or if it happen, it gives you no security. It is an ignoble resource, since it does not depend on you for its success; and those modes of defence are alone good, certain and lasting, which depend upon yourself and your own worth.

Chapter XXV.

What Fortune Can Effect in Human Affairs, and How She May Be Withstood

I am not ignorant that many have been and are of the opinion that human affairs are so governed by Fortune and by God, that men cannot alter them by any prudence of theirs, and indeed have no remedy against them, and for this reason have come to think that it is not worthwhile to labour much about anything, but that they must leave everything to be determined by chance.

Often when I turn the matter over, I am in part inclined to agree with this opinion, which has had the readier acceptance in our own times from the great changes in things which we have seen, and every day see happen contrary to all human expectation. Nevertheless, that our free will be not wholly set aside, I think it may be the case that Fortune is the mistress of one half our actions, and yet leaves the control of the other half, or a little less, to ourselves. And I would liken her to one of those wild torrents which, when angry, overflow the plains, sweep away trees and houses, and carry off soil from one bank to throw it down upon the other. Every one flees before them, and yields to their fury without the least power to resist. And yet, though this be their nature, it does not follow that in seasons of fair weather, men cannot, by constructing weirs and moles, take such precautions as will cause them when again in flood to pass off by some artificial channel, or at least prevent their course from being so uncontrolled and destructive. And so it is with Fortune, who displays her might where there is no organized strength to resist her, and directs her onset where she knows that there is neither barrier nor embankment to confine her.

And if you look at Italy, which has been at once the seat of these changes and their cause, you will perceive that it is a field without embankment or barrier. For if, like Germany, France, and Spain, it had been guarded with sufficient skill, this inundation, if it ever came upon us, would never have wrought the violent changes which we have witnessed.

This I think enough to say generally touching resistance to Fortune. But confining myself more closely to the matter in hand, I note that one day we see a Prince prospering and the next day overthrown, without detecting any change in his nature or character. This, I believe, comes chiefly from a cause already dwelt upon, namely, that a Prince who rests wholly on Fortune is ruined when she changes. Moreover, I believe that he will prosper most whose mode of acting best adapts itself to the character of the times; and conversely that he will be unprosperous, with whose mode of acting the times do not accord. For we see that men in these matters which lead to the end that each has before him, namely, glory and wealth, proceed by different ways, one with caution, another with impetuosity, one with violence, another with subtlety, one with patience, another with its contrary; and that by one or other of these different courses each may succeed.

Again, of two who act cautiously, you shall find that one attains his end, the other not, and that two of different temperament, the one cautious, the other impetuous, are equally successful. All which happens from no other cause than that the character of the times accords or does not accord with their methods of acting. And hence it comes, as I have already said, that two operating differently arrive at the same result, and two operating similarly, the one succeeds and the other not. On this likewise depend the vicissitudes of Fortune. For if to one who conducts himself with caution and patience, time and circumstances are propitious, so that his method of acting is good, he goes on prospering; but if these change he is ruined, because he does not change his method of acting.

For no man is found so prudent as to know how to adapt himself to these changes, both because he cannot deviate from the course to which nature inclines him, and because, having always prospered while adhering to one path, he cannot be persuaded that it would be well for him to forsake it. And so when occasion requires the cautious man to act impetuously, he cannot do so and is undone: whereas, had he changed his nature with time and circumstances, his fortune would have been unchanged.

Pope Julius II proceeded with impetuosity in all his undertakings, and found time and circumstances in such harmony with his mode of acting that he always obtained a happy result. Witness his first expedition against Bologna, when Messer Giovanni Bentivoglio was yet living. The Venetians were not favourable to the enterprise; nor was the King of Spain. Negotiations respecting it with the King of France were still open. Nevertheless, the Pope with his wonted hardihood and impetuosity marched in person on the expedition, and by this movement brought the King of Spain and the Venetians to a check, the latter through fear, the former from his eagerness to recover the entire Kingdom of Naples; at the same time, he dragged after him the King of France, who, desiring to have the Pope for an ally in humbling the Venetians, on finding him already in motion saw that he could not refuse him his soldiers without openly offending him. By the impetuosity of his movements, therefore, Julius effected what no other Pontiff endowed with the highest human prudence could. For had he, as any other Pope would have done, put off his departure from Rome until terms had been settled and everything duly arranged, he never would have succeeded. For the King of France would have found a thousand pretexts to delay him, and the others would have menaced him with a thousand alarms. I shall not touch upon his other actions, which were all of a like character, and all of which had a happy issue, since the shortness of his life did not allow him to experience reverses. But if times had overtaken him, rendering a cautious line of conduct necessary, his ruin must have ensued, since he never could have departed from those methods to which nature inclined him.

To be brief, I say that since Fortune changes and men stand fixed in their old ways, they are prosperous so long as there is congruity between them, and the reverse when there is not. Of this, however, I am well persuaded, that it is better to be impetuous than cautious. For Fortune is a woman who to be kept under must be beaten and roughly handled; and we see that she suffers herself to be more readily mastered by those who so treat her than by those who are more timid in their approaches. And always, like a woman, she favours the young, because they are less scrupulous and fiercer, and command her with greater audacity.

Chapter XXVI.

An Exhortation to Liberate Italy from the Barbarians

Turning over in my mind all the matters which have above been considered, and debating with myself whether in Italy at the present hour the times are such as might serve to confer honour on a new Prince, and whether a fit opportunity now offers for a prudent and valiant leader to bring about changes glorious for himself and beneficial to the whole Italian people, it seems to me that so many conditions combine to further such an enterprise, that I know of no time so favourable to it as the present. And if, as I have said, it was necessary in order to display the valour of Moses that the children of Israel should be slaves in Egypt, and to know the greatness and courage of Cyrus that the Persians should be oppressed by the Medes, and to illustrate the excellence of Theseus that the Athenians should be scattered and divided, so at this hour, to prove the worth of some Italian hero, it was required that Italy should be brought to her present abject condition, to be more a slave than the Hebrew, more oppressed than the Persian, more disunited than the Athenian, without a head, without order, beaten, spoiled, torn in pieces, over-run and abandoned to destruction in every shape.

But though, heretofore, glimmerings may have been discerned in this man or that, whence it might be conjectured that he was ordained by God for her redemption, nevertheless it has afterwards been seen in the further course of his actions that Fortune has disowned him; so that our country, left almost without life, still waits to know who it is that is to heal her bruises, to put an end to the devastation and plunder of Lombardy, to the exactions and imposts of Naples and Tuscany, and to stanch those wounds of hers which long neglect has changed into running sores.

We see how she prays God to send someone to rescue her from these barbarous cruelties and oppressions. We see too how ready and eager she is to follow any standard were there only someone to raise it. But at present we see no one except in your illustrious House (pre-eminent by its virtues and good fortune, and favoured by God and by the Church whose headship it now holds), who could undertake the part of a deliverer.

But for you this will not be too hard a task, if you keep before your eyes the lives and actions of those whom I have named above. For although these men were singular and extraordinary, after all they were but men, not one of whom had so great an opportunity as now presents itself to you. For their undertakings were not more just than this, nor more easy, nor was God more their friend than yours. The justice of the cause is conspicuous; for that war is just which is necessary, and those arms are sacred from which we derive our only hope. Everywhere there is the strongest disposition to engage in this cause; and where the disposition is strong the difficulty cannot be great, provided you follow the methods observed by those whom I have set before you as models.

But further, we see here extraordinary and unexampled proofs of Divine favour. The sea has been divided; the cloud has attended you on your way; the rock has flowed with water; the manna has rained from heaven; everything has concurred to promote your greatness. What remains to be done must be done by you; since in order not to deprive us of our free will and such share of glory as belongs to us, God will not do everything himself.

Nor is to be marvelled at if none of those Italians I have named has been able to effect what we hope to see effected by your illustrious House; or that amid so many revolutions and so many warlike movements it should always appear as though the military virtues of Italy were spent; for this comes her old system being defective, and from no one being found among us capable to strike out a new. Nothing confers such honour on the reformer of a State, as do the new laws and institutions which he devises; for these when they stand on a solid basis and have a greatness in their scope, make him admired and venerated. And in Italy material is not wanting for improvement in every form. If the head be weak the limbs are strong, and we see daily in single combats, or where few are engaged, how superior are the strength, dexterity, and intelligence of Italians. But when it comes to armies, they are nowhere, and this from no other reason than the defects of their leaders. For those who are skillful in arms will not obey, and everyone thinks himself skillful, since hitherto we have had none among us so raised by merit or by fortune above his fellows that they should yield him the palm. And hence it happens that for the long period of twenty years, during which so many wars have taken place, whenever there has been an army purely Italian it has always been beaten. To this testify, first Taro, then Alessandria, Capua, Genoa, Vaila, Bologna, Mestri.

If then your illustrious House should seek to follow the example of those great men who have delivered their country in past ages, it is before all things necessary, as the true foundation of every such attempt, to be provided with national troops, since you can have no braver, truer, or more faithful soldiers; and although every single man of them be good, collectively they will be better, seeing themselves commanded by their own Prince, and honoured and esteemed by him. That you may be able, therefore, to defend yourself against the foreigner with Italian valour, the first step is to provide yourself with an army such as this.

And although the Swiss and the Spanish infantry are each esteemed formidable, there are yet defects in both, by reason of which troops trained on a different system might not merely withstand them, but be certain of defeating them. For the Spaniards cannot resist cavalry and the Swiss will give way before infantry if they find them as resolute as themselves at close quarters. Whence it has been seen, and may be seen again, that the Spaniards cannot sustain the onset of the French men-at-arms and that the Swiss are broken by the Spanish foot. And although of this last we have no complete instance, we have yet an indication of it in the battle of Ravenna, where the Spanish infantry confronted the German companies who have the same discipline as the Swiss; on which occasion the Spaniards by their agility and with the aid of their bucklers forced their way under the pikes, and stood ready to close with the Germans, who were no longer in a position to defend themselves; and had they not been charged by cavalry, they must have put the Germans to utter rout. Knowing, then, the defects of each of these kinds of troops, you can train your men on some different system, to withstand cavalry and not to fear infantry. To effect this, will not require the creation of any new forces, but simply a change in the discipline of the old. And these are matters in reforming which the new Prince acquires reputation and importance.

This opportunity then, for Italy at last to look on her deliverer, ought not to be allowed to pass away. With what love he would be received in all those Provinces which have suffered from the foreign inundation, with what thirst for vengeance, with what fixed fidelity, with what devotion, and what tears, no words of mine can declare. What gates would be closed against him? What people would refuse him obedience? What jealousy would stand in his way? What Italian but would yield him homage? This barbarian tyranny stinks in all nostrils.

Let your illustrious House therefore take upon itself this enterprise with all the courage and all the hopes with which a just cause is undertaken; so that under your standard this our country may be ennobled, and under your auspices be fulfilled the words of Petrarch:—

> Brief will be the strife
> When valour arms against barbaric rage;
> For the bold spirit of the bygone age
> Still warms Italian hearts with life.

Petrarch, Canz. XVI, V. 93-96

THE END